1939

The Making of Six
Great Films from Hollywood's
Greatest Year

Charles F. Adams

CRAVEN
STREET
B O O K S

Fresno, California

1939: The Making of Six Great Films from Hollywood's Greatest Year
Copyright ©2014 by Charles F. Adams. All rights reserved.

Published by Craven Street Books
An imprint of Linden Publishing
2006 South Mary Street, Fresno, California 93721
(559) 233-6633 / (800) 345-4447

Cover and interior design by Maura J. Zimmer

CravenStreetBooks.com
Craven Street Books and Colophon are trademarks of Linden Publishing, Inc.

ISBN 978-1-61035-197-3

135798642

Printed in the United States of America on acid-free paper.

Library of Congress Cataloging-in-Publication Data

Adams, Charles F. (Charles Francis), 1927-
 1939 : the making of six great films from Hollywood's greatest year / by Charles F. Adams.
  pages cm
 ISBN 978-1-61035-197-3 (pbk.)
 1. Motion pictures--United States--History--20th century. I. Title. II. Title: Nineteen thirty-nine.

PN1993.5.U6A33 2013
791.43'0973'09044--dc23

2013025793

MIX
Paper from
responsible sources
FSC® C011935
FSC
www.fsc.org

TABLE OF CONTENTS

AUTHOR'S NOTE

When I was twelve years old, going to the movies was a Saturday afternoon ritual that my friends and I observed with an almost religious fervor. We went because there wasn't much else to do on Saturday afternoon, because we knew that all the other kids in town would be there, and because it didn't cost much. The first showing was called a "children's matinee," and while we preferred not to think of ourselves as children, we were willing to suffer the indignity because the price was right: ten cents.

There was only one theater in town so choice was not a problem. It was important to arrive early because there could be as many as a hundred kids standing in line, noisily jostling for position. If someone tried to sneak into the front of the line, they would be admonished with yells of "No cuts, no cuts!" Because the price of ten cents was available only to those "twelve and under," the theater manager would stand near the head of the line to weed out any malefactors who approached the box office "walking low" to disguise their age and avoid paying twenty-five cents. Sometimes there were arguments.

Once you put down your dime, the lady behind the glass window gave you a ticket stub and you proceeded into the theater, making a mandatory stop at the concession stand. I always bought Black Crows, which cost more than the theater ticket. When you entered the theater itself you were confronted with a scene that teetered between bedlam and chaos. Because there were never, ever any adults present, everyone celebrated this fleeting freedom by yelling at friends, making jokes, and running up and down the aisle. Not infrequently there was racing. If the movie was late in starting, which it almost always was, we would stomp our feet in a display of dissatisfaction. When the lights were finally lowered and the stage curtain parted, there was always cheering, whistling, and applause.

We had not come just to see a movie. We came to see the movies! First there would be a newsreel showing us all the important events of the week that none of us cared about. Next would come a cartoon which was always greeted with shouts of approval. Then the first movie came on. We all knew that this was the "B" movie, the main purpose of which was to permit the theater to advertise that it was showing a "double feature." We usually didn't recognize any of the actors in the first movie, unless it was Chester Morris playing "Boston Blackie" or Roy Rogers playing "Roy Rogers." It served the useful purpose of having the theater settle down, with the occasional catcall or wisecrack sapping the last of our disruptive energies. Then came the "A" movie, the feature film, and we often learned for the first time what it was when the title came on because we hadn't paid any attention to the marquee outside. By this time we were settled in for the long haul, paid reasonable attention for the next ninety minutes, and finally left the theater feeling entertained and happy.

I probably saw almost all of the major films in 1939 because, unless I was sick and in bed, I went to the movies every Saturday afternoon. And despite the environment in which I saw them, I remember some scenes from these movies with surprising clarity—Huckleberry Finn sprinkling ketchup on the ground to fake his death, Scarlett O'Hara threading her way through the dead and wounded bodies in Atlanta, Sherlock Holmes doing battle with that great, fearsome hound, Dorothy suddenly going from black and white to color, Jimmy Stewart falling to the floor in the Senate, John Wayne leaping from horse to horse to stop the stagecoach. We didn't think about nor did we care how those images got on the screen, although the faint hum of the projector suggested that machinery was involved.

But now I do know. Each of these movies has its own remarkable history—how the original story was written, how it was translated into a movie script, where the money came from, how the actors were chosen, how the directors managed to put it all together.

These stories are, by and large, quite amazing. But the most amazing thing, at least to me, is that they all happened seventy-five years ago. The passage of the years has not dimmed my affection for the movies of my childhood. Chronicling the six of them found in this book, all from the movie year I remember best, has been both a challenge and a delight—much like researching and writing the biographies of six old friends. Now I feel that I know them even better, and appreciate them so much more.

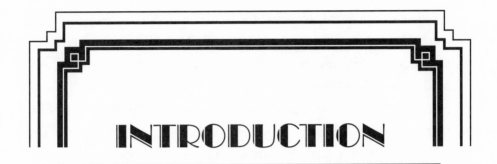

INTRODUCTION

Film critics and historians are virtually unanimous in considering 1939 the greatest year in the history of motion pictures—and with good reason. The number of memorable and legendary films produced in that year is astonishing—*Gone With the Wind, The Wizard of Oz, Goodbye, Mr. Chips, Stagecoach, Wuthering Heights, The Adventures of Huckleberry Finn, The Hound of the Baskervilles, Ninotchka, The Hunchback of Notre Dame, Gunga Din, Of Mice and Men, Dark Victory,* and *Mr. Smith Goes to Washington.* There have been other outstanding movie years since, but none with the overwhelming credentials of 1939.

It was a rare confluence of circumstances and events that made it such a productive year for Hollywood. This was the era of the big studios: MGM, Twentieth Century Fox, Paramount, RKO, and Warner Brothers—and they had at their disposal an amazing array of talent. They employed more than a hundred directors, including John Ford, King Vidor, William Wyler, Victor Fleming, and Cecil B. DeMille. The writing staffs of these studios were virtually a "Who's Who" of American writers, including Ben Hecht, Nathaniel West, William Faulkner, and F. Scott Fitzgerald. The list of movie stars on their payrolls included names that still echo down through the decades—Cary Grant, Joan Crawford, Bette Davis, Fred Astaire, Ginger Rogers, James Cagney, Jimmy Stewart, Errol Flynn, Judy Garland, Greta Garbo, Henry Fonda, Katharine Hepburn, Spencer Tracy, Clark Gable.

This vast talent pool was at the beck and call of the studios. For the most part, these star-quality actors and actresses were employees in every sense of the word, required to do whatever was asked of them at whatever time the studios wanted them to do it. They were told what movies they would work on and be in, what their salaries would be, and when they would be "loaned" out to other studios.

And the studios worked them hard. In 1939, the American film industry produced 365 feature films, a remarkable rate of one movie per day. The studios were feeding a greedy audience of theater-goers across the country who couldn't get enough of the Hollywood product. In the late 1930s, more than fifty million people went to the movies at least once a week, spending over 80 percent of their entertainment dollars on theater tickets. Understandably, theater owners were insatiable in their demands for an ongoing stream of quality films, changing their marquees two or three times a week. Hollywood was more than happy to oblige.

Ironically, all this was happening at the depths of the Great Depression, with the prospect of war looming over the country. Hollywood was taking on the job of entertaining a disheartened people—of making them forget their problems for a time—of lifting their spirits and inspiring their hopes. And, while they were doing that, the studios were also in the process of making lots of money. The average motion picture produced in 1939 cost just over $300,000—and it brought in twice that amount. As a result, the country's moneymen were eager to invest in films, virtually guaranteeing themselves a more than satisfactory return. The availability of funds meant that studios were seldom without the resources they needed for films they wanted to produce.

The year 1939 was also a time of great advancement in the technology of making films. Sound recording was better, film was faster, cameras were more mobile and flexible, rear projection had been mastered, and pictures could now be made in full color. The Technicolor process had first been used in a few films at the start of the decade, but it had recently made a giant leap forward with what was called the "three-strip process," permitting pictures to be made in full, brilliant color. Two of the year's greatest films would take advantage of this achievement.

If the 1930s and 1940s marked the Golden Age of Cinema, surely 1939 was the epicenter of that age. Happily for theater lovers, the year lives on today, not just in movie houses, but also on television and on computer screens. Like Oz's Yellow Brick Road, the classic movies of 1939 still glisten like gold for all to see.

GONE WITH the WIND

by MARGARET MITCHELL

GONE WITH THE WIND

The Story

In the late autumn of 1935, book editor Harold Latham sat at his desk in the Manhattan offices of Macmillan Publishers, looking at a disorganized six-inch pile of paper resting on his desk. This was not the carefully typed and arranged manuscript he was accustomed to dealing with. Some of the pages were typewritten, others were handwritten. Text cross-outs and extensive margin notes littered the pages. There were various kinds and sizes of paper in the pile, including packaging paper and even several envelopes. Latham realized that tackling this manuscript submission would be a formidable undertaking. He had already peered into the pile of more than 1,200 pages enough to realize that it had no first chapter. The top page gave little clue as to its contents. It stated simply: "Tomorrow Is Another Day."

A short time earlier, Latham had been in Atlanta on a scouting expedition, looking for new writers of Southern fiction. At a luncheon given by a bookstore owner, Latham was introduced to a petite, charming woman named Peggy Marsh. They struck up an instant friendship and met several times before the editor brought up a rumor he had heard that she was herself writing a novel. She denied it, and her denial was, in

left: **The original front cover**
of *Gone with the Wind*

Peggy Marsh

fact, the truth. She had started writing a story four years earlier about life in the South at the time of the Civil War, but she said she was no longer working on it. She had started writing out of boredom after a sprained ankle had confined her to her house. She had no real plot in mind and actually wrote the last chapter first. Then, over the years, she kept adding to the story, writing events out of sequence and stuffing chapters, finished and unfinished, into envelopes that she sequestered around the house. Her heroine was named Pansy O'Hara and she lived in a large house called Fontenoy Hall. Her hero was Rhett Butler.

At first, she called her book *Bugles Rang True*, later changing it to *Tote the Weary Load*. After several years of off-and–on work, she abandoned the project altogether, and her disassembled novel remained hidden in various desks and closets. Only her husband had any real clue as to the existence of Peggy's novel, and when he learned that a publisher's representative had expressed interest, he convinced her to round up the scattered pieces of her work and put them in some kind of order.

The night before Latham was scheduled to leave Atlanta, he received a phone call in his hotel room. It was Peggy, asking if he could come down to the lobby. She had something to show him. Latham went down and found her sitting by herself on a hotel couch. Next to her rested a veritable mountain of paper wrapped in string. The next morning, Latham purchased an extra suitcase to carry the huge bundle of pages back to New York.

Back in his office, Latham perused the pages he had carefully loaded and carried back from Georgia, and he soon realized he was holding something special in his hands. The story had scope, history, sweep, and grandeur. The characters seemed to leap off the pages, taking on a life and breath of their own. Pansy O'Hara was now a beautiful, fiery, selfish young woman now named Scarlett O'Hara. Rhett Butler was bigger than life, handsome, debonair, charming, clever, and devious. Latham put the manuscript back on his table, next to a telegram from Peggy Marsh that had arrived earlier and had awaited him on his return. It read: "Send the manuscript back. I have changed my mind." Latham decided to ignore the wire, and

Peggy Marsh at her writing desk

instead he sent Peggy a publisher's contract with a $250 advance. When it arrived in Atlanta, Peggy was both flattered and chagrined. She didn't really want to sign it and take on the responsibility of completing the novel. Fortunately for motion picture history, her husband changed her mind.

For the next six months, Peggy labored over her novel, reorganizing it, sharpening its characters, and checking historical details. She became so devoted to perfecting her novel that she re-wrote the previously missing first chapter more than seventy times. And, at last, she decided on a title. She would call it *Gone with the Wind*, inspired by a poem she had recently read by Ernest Dowson that included the line: "I have forgot much, Cynera. Gone with the wind!"

She also decided to use her maiden name as her *nom de plume*. In Atlanta, she was known as Peggy Marsh. As an author, she would be known as Margaret Mitchell.

The Movie Sale

The finished manuscript arrived at Macmillan in the early winter of 1936. Latham was thrilled with the final product and confident he had a best seller on his hands. The executives at Macmillan agreed with Latham's enthusiasm, but they decided to hedge their bet: They wanted a prepublication movie sale.

The assignment went to Annie Laurie Williams, one of the best literary agents in the business. Williams had already earned a reputation for selling books and scripts to the movie industry, and she had access to all of the major story editors in Hollywood.

After reading the novel, Williams was even more enthusiastic than her male associates at Macmillan. Armed with advance galley proofs and a carefully constructed synopsis, she began to make her rounds. To her surprise, she ran into a number of unforeseen obstacles. Recent popular books had not translated into moneymaking films. Additionally, studio executives were not looking kindly on period movies. Films like *Mutiny on the Bounty* and *A Tale of Two Cities* had recently bombed at the box office. As one producer decreed: "No more feather pens!"

Louis B. Mayer was the most important and powerful man in Hollywood. His decisions, even his whims, made and broke producers, directors, and stars. It was his habit not to read scripts but to listen to them. His assistant, Kate Korbaly, combed through scripts and stories that she thought worthy, then told the stories to Mayer in his office. Korbaly loved *Gone with the Wind*. She relayed the story in great detail for Mayer, evoking as much emotion and enthusiasm as she could muster. Mayer listened patiently for almost an hour, then waved his hand to indicate he had heard enough. Civil War; selfish heroine; scheming war profiteer; hints of misogyny and interracial coupling; no happy ending.

Louis B. Mayer

Mayer was not interested. He would let some other studio lose its money on this novel by an unknown author.

Warner Brothers was Annie Williams' next target. Warner director Mervyn LeRoy's daughter read a synopsis of the novel on the strength of LeRoy's wife's recommendation. She read the advance proofs, loved the story, and encouraged her father to take it to studio head Jack Warner. LeRoy passed it along to Warner with the suggestion they might buy the novel if their leading star, Bette Davis, would take the role of Scarlett. Warner, in turn, tried to interest Davis. She turned it down cold.

Next Williams tried to interest Lily Messinger, script editor at RKO. Messinger pored over the pages with mounting enthusiasm. She loved everything about *Gone with the Wind*—the sweeping drama, the spectacular Scarlett character, and, most of all, the unforgettable Rhett Butler. She sent it along to Pandro Berman, RKO's number-one producer. All Berman could see were the problems, especially the huge cost of producing what would surely be one of the most expensive films of all time.

A pattern was emerging. *Gone with the Wind* seemed to enrapture almost every woman who read it. Men who read it were far less enthusiastic. Williams began to wonder if this might be what was called a "ladies' book" and not have the broad appeal necessary for a best seller. But she was determined to keep fighting for it. She took it to David O. Selznick.

Williams' avenue to Selznick was through Kay Brown, the story editor for International Pictures, the independent film company that Selznick had established just a year earlier. The pattern repeated itself: Kay Brown read the novel and was simply overwhelmed by it. She sent the novel to her boss with an urgent plea to buy the film rights. Her telegram left no doubts: "I beg, urge, coax, and plead

David O. Selznick

with you to read this at once ... drop everything and buy it." Selznick's response: Silence. Brown prodded her boss again and finally received a telegram: "Sorry to say no, despite your enthusiasm."

Macmillan published *Gone with the Wind* in May of 1936. It was long: 1,037 pages. The critics were overwhelming in their praise. *New York Times* critic J. Donald Adams wrote: "It is, in its narrative power, in sheer readability, surpassed by nothing in American fiction." The *New York Post* called it "profoundly stirring." Critic Robert Nation remarked, "at 1,037 pages, the three best novels I have read this year." Within one month, *Gone with the Wind* sold 176,000 copies. Three weeks later, there were more than 300,000 copies in the hands of readers across the country. Suddenly, everyone wanted the book—including Hollywood.

Selznick quickly offered $50,000 for the movie rights, and the offer was just as quickly accepted. Half of the money went to publisher Macmillan and half to author Mitchell. It was the highest amount ever paid for film rights to a work of fiction. Not content with having paid such an extraordinary amount, Selznick leaked word to gossip columnist Louella Parsons that he had paid $65,000.

It was just the beginning of the Hollywood hype that would surround the filming of *Gone with the Wind* during the years ahead.

Putting the Team Together

In the fall of 1936, Selznick assembled the carefully chosen crew he had put together to bring *Gone with the Wind* to the screen. Each crew member brought with him a time-tested talent, as well as his own personal prejudices toward the project.

Henry Guisberg was Selznick's money man. He was basically opposed to the whole project. He had warned Selznick early on that it could bring him to financial ruin. The cost of production, he felt, was far beyond the capacity of an independent studio.

George Cukor was selected to direct the film. Cukor was a veteran Selznick director and one of the most influential and honored directors in Hollywood. He seemed an ideal choice. He had a superb track record of turning out successful and profitable films, including *Dinner at Eight*, *Little Women*, and *David Copperfield*. Moreover, he had a long history of working with Selznick. His reputation for coaxing top-notch performances from female stars was also in his favor, as the roles of both Scarlett and Melanie would be critical to the film's success.

Walter Plunkett, one of the top stylists in Hollywood, would be in charge of costumes—and he would have his hands full on this complicated period project. Lee Garmes, one of the industry's top cameramen, would see that all the action was recorded on film.

FINDING THE RIGHT RHETT

From the first time Selznick read the novel, he had envisioned Clark Gable in the role of Rhett Butler. So did hundreds of thousands of women who read the book. So did most of Hollywood and even most of Gable's friends. Gable was even frequently addressed at MGM as "Rhett" in the studio commissary. Certainly Gable seemed tailor-made for the role. Ruggedly handsome, debonair, strong featured, and well built, he was at the peak of his powers and his popularity. Ever since his Academy Award performance in *It Happened One Night*, Gable had been an American icon. Moviegoers simply couldn't get enough of Gable. Since the start of the decade, he had starred in thirty-eight movies and was annually voted filmdom's top box office attraction. And Gable was considered a "man's man." Sam Goldwyn once said, "When someone like Robert Montgomery comes on the screen, you know he has *cojones*. When Gable comes on, you can hear them clanging." In the hearts of the country's women, and in the hearts of Hollywood's money men, Gable was simply "The King."

However, other Hollywood actors were keen on playing Rhett. Ronald Colman, one of the industry's top stars, coveted the role. He campaigned heartily in person and in print and even told Selznick that he was willing to live in Atlanta for several months to turn his elegant British accent into a soft Southern drawl. Gossip columnists advocated briefly for Errol Flynn, the wondrously handsome actor from Down Under, whose recent appearance as Robin Hood was making ladies' hearts across the nation flutter. Selznick briefly considered Flynn but eventually decided the Tasmanian actor did not have sufficient acting chops to sustain the role. George Brent, a handsome, mustachioed, "B"

The young Gable at his masculine best

movie actor, campaigned for the role and was briefly considered—but only briefly. Gary Cooper, Gable's only real competitor for top stardom in Hollywood, was eager to play Rhett, but his contract with another studio would not permit it.

British actor Basil Rathbone read *Gone with the Wind* and concluded that he would be the perfect Rhett Butler. He made overtures but received no encouragement, but would go on the next year to star in another film that was tailor-made to his talents and that would cement his image in the public mind as the world's first and greatest private detective.

Margaret Mitchell, who had declared earlier that she did not want to participate in the making of the film, confirmed the wisdom of her decision with her own personal recommendation for the role of Rhett Butler: Groucho Marx.

And so, finally, it became clear that Selznick would have to get Gable. Selznick wanted him, Hollywood favored him, and the public virtually demanded him. However, Gable was not available to the Selznick studios. He was under contract to Metro-Goldwyn-Mayer, and Louis B. Mayer, MGM's sole ruler, saw no virtue in lending out his greatest star to Selznick. When Selznick inquired what it would take to get Gable, he learned that the price would be full and exclusive distribution rights to *Gone with the Wind*. That was unacceptable.

Eventually, however, public pressure dictated that MGM and Selznick negotiate. The two studios finally worked out an arrangement whereby MGM would lend Selznick its star and contribute $1,250,000 toward production of the film, in exchange for distribution rights and a sliding scale of the film's gross profits.

By this time, book sales of *Gone with the Wind* had soared to more than one million. It seemed that everyone had read or was reading the novel—everyone, that is, except Clark Gable.

With Hollywood columnists speculating almost daily that Gable would be Rhett—with friends, associates, and even carparkers calling him "Rhett"—it is perplexing that Gable had not gotten around to reading the novel. Perhaps Gable was just not a reader. It was well known that he spent his weekends fishing and hunting with friends— and his evenings and nights with Carole Lombard.

Both Mayer and Selznick encouraged Gable to read the novel, and he reluctantly took it with him on a long weekend trip. When he returned, he astonished both moguls by announcing that he wanted

Gable pretending to read *Gone with the Wind*

nothing to do with Rhett Butler. It wasn't his kind of role. He couldn't act properly using a Southern accent.

But this was the era of studio tyranny. Even the biggest stars were arbitrarily assigned roles and were expected to do their best even with scripts that displeased them. Still, Gable needed some added inducement, and Mayer found it. He learned that Gable needed some quick cash in order to divorce his wife, Ria Langham—and that Lombard was getting impatient. He offered Gable a $100,000 bonus to look kindly on the role of Rhett Butler. It was a veritable fortune—and Gable took it. In June of 1937, with Selznick and Mayer in attendance, Gable signed the contract for the role of Rhett Butler.

Next, another problem with Gable arose. He still had obligations to act in other films at MGM that would preclude his starting on *Gone with the Wind* at any time during the upcoming year and a half. Selznick decided he couldn't wait that long to start filming. He decided to stoke

Gable signing his contract with Selznick and MGM

the publicity fires by proceeding immediately with the filming of one of the most dramatic scenes in the novel.

THE GREAT FIRE

It was obvious to observers on the evening of December 10, 1937, that the Selznick studios were burning down. Fire engines sprang into action and motorists jammed the streets to witness the catastrophe. But what they were actually witnessing was the burning of Atlanta.

The back lots at Selznick studios had been crammed with old and useless sets from such earlier productions as *Little Lord Fauntleroy* and *King Kong*. The area would have to be cleared for the construction of new *Gone with the Wind* sets, and the Selznick team had come up with a novel way to get rid of the old sets while at the same time getting the filming of the new picture under way. After putting some new fronts on the old sets, crew members set the whole area on fire while doubles for

Scarlett and Rhett ran in and out of the scene. The burning of Atlanta, one of the key scenes in the Mitchell novel, was in the can.

THE SEARCH FOR SCARLETT

With Gable signed but not yet available, Selznick had more time to fill in what was perhaps the next most important piece of the puzzle: casting the role of Scarlett O'Hara. The search had been going on full blast for almost a year.

Readers of Mitchell's novel were enthralled with this new heroine. She was beautiful, self-centered, and wildly self-assured: "The green eyes in her sweet face were turbulent, lusty with life, instinctively at variance with her decorous demeanor." Women wanted to be her and men just wanted her. And it seemed that every movie star, every model, and every Hollywood hopeful wanted to play her on the screen.

Bette Davis had first had a chance at the role, but she had turned it down haughtily without really knowing much about it. Then she read the book and quickly changed her mind. However, now Selznick didn't want her. Katharine Hepburn had been quick out of the starting gates. She had read *Gone with the Wind* in galley proofs and concluded without reservation that she should play Scarlett. She appealed personally to Selznick, who ended her hopes with one withering sentence: "I can't imagine Rhett Butler pursuing you for ten years."

There followed a long procession of hopefuls. Almost every female actress under forty seemed to covet the role. Many of them, although lacking any real enthusiasm on Selznick's part, were important enough or sufficiently well connected to demand a screen test: Joan Crawford, Jean Arthur, Joan Bennett, Tallulah Bankhead, Paulette Goddard, and Lana Turner. Perhaps because filming was some time off or because he wanted to crank up publicity for the film, Selznick announced he wanted a new, fresh, untried actress to play Scarlett. To achieve this, a national search would be conducted, concentrated in the American South. Talent scouts and publicity agents were dispatched to universities, modeling agencies, and local acting studios. The result was near chaos as young ladies of every stripe and description rushed to fill the void. Some were interviewed, a few auditioned, fewer still were dispatched to California

To: Mr. Birdwell

Subject: GONE WITH THE WIND -statement

Date: 1/10/38

Dear Russell:

Please prepare a statement for me along the following lines (this in order to pave the way for selection of a known actress for Scarlett, in case we are forced to it):

"I am reaching the end of my rope on a search for a new girl to play Scarlett O'Hara. We have gone to great extremes of effort and expenditure to find such a girl, but I am frankly almost willing to admit now that I have bitten off more than I can chew and that the search for Scarlett is not likely to be as successful as the search for Tom Sawyer, if only because of the requirements of youth and enormous acting talent, which in themselves are contradictory because of the lack of experience in newcomers and girls of the right age. I am setting myself a deadline and if within it we do not find a new girl, we will select a known actress."

DICTATED BUT NOT READ BY
DAVID O. SELZNICK

Selznick memo on the search for Scarlett O'Hara

Paulette Goddard

for screen tests. Pretty young ladies, lusting to be Scarlett, showed up every morning at the Selznick studios trying to stoke someone's attention. One candidate even had herself delivered to Selznick in a box. Before it was over, more than 1,500 women had been interviewed, and 160,000 feet of black-and-white film had been expended on fifty-nine possible Scarletts. More than twice the amount originally spent on the purchase of the film rights had been lavished on the search for a "fresh, unknown actress to play Scarlett." When it was all over, Selznick decided he didn't want a "fresh, untested" actress. Instead, he wanted a known actress, familiar to the moviegoing public. Scarlett O'Hara would be Paulette Goddard.

Young, beautiful, and talented, Goddard had been brilliant in her screen test. She had shown the kind of spunk and fire that Selznick was looking for. Selznick put Goddard under a five-year contract and dispatched her to New Orleans with a voice coach. He let the word leak out via Louella Parsons' column to a waiting and grateful world: Goddard had been signed to play Scarlett. Parsons' column went on to describe Goddard as a talented actress and the constant companion of Charlie Chaplin.

Unfortunately, the wording of Parsons' column caused a problem. "Constant companion" was Hollywood code for "living in sin." Everyone knew that Goddard and Chaplin were a couple, living together and traveling and entertaining as man and wife. There had long been an assumption that they were married, and it was an illusion they did their best to publicly promote. This was the era of artificial morality in movietown. The Hayes Office, arbiter of film standards, rode roughshod over scripts, eliminating swearing and timing movie kisses with a stopwatch. Studios saw to it that their stars did not get unsavory publicity, that their lives were portrayed as clean, sober, and family oriented.

Selznick began to get letters condemning Goddard for her lifestyle. Moralists and even preachers started questioning his choice of Goddard to play the most important movie role of the era. Sensing the possibility of a scandal, Selznick asked Paulette Goddard to come in with her wedding license. When she came in empty handed, Selznick fired her. The search for Scarlett was back on the burner.

This time, however, the search would not take long. At a Hollywood gathering just a few weeks following the Goddard debacle, Selznick's brother Myron tapped him on the shoulder and said, "David, I'd like you to meet Vivien Leigh." As Selznick recalled later, "I turned and suddenly found myself staring into the eyes of Scarlett O'Hara." This was no doubt a romanticized version of the actual event, but Selznick was certainly impressed with what he saw. Leigh was a stunning beauty, with deep auburn hair and sparkling gray-green eyes. She had been in a number of English films and had been a hit on the London stage. More famously, she was having a celebrated affair with the great British actor Laurence Olivier. Surprisingly, this did not overly concern Selznick. Apparently, continental sex was not as worrisome as the domestic variety. Could an English actress achieve a believable Southern accent? Of course, she could. As a trained and talented actress, Leigh could probably have done a French accent with Hungarian overtones. She tested perfectly and Selznick was quick to confirm publicly that Vivien Leigh would be Scarlett O'Hara. Photos of the signing ceremony were flashed to a waiting world.

Casting for the remaining roles was completed with relative dispatch, although some of the actors signed on with reservations. Leslie Howard accepted the role of the hapless Ashley Wilkes, despite his fear of being typecast as a weak character. The role of Melanie, Scarlett's rival in matters of love, went to Olivia de Havilland, despite her knowing

The face that convinced Selznick he had found his Scarlett

that the part had first been offered to her sister, Joan Fontaine, and despite being told by Jack Warner, "You don't want to be in that movie… it will be the biggest bust ever." Character actor Thomas Mitchell signed as Scarlett's father, even though he was afraid of horses and had a clause inserted in his contract that he didn't have to ride one. (He did—when the time came.) Evelyn Keyes accepted Selznick's invitation to play Scarlett's sister, despite having turned down an earlier invitation to join Selznick on the casting coach. (She escaped by dodging nimbly around his office with Selznick in pursuit.)

Vivien Leigh signing her contract with MGM

Selznick had a brilliant idea for casting Belle Watling, the prostitute: Mae West. West was interested, but only if she could write her own lines. That was not acceptable and Selznick finally gave the role to a virtual unknown, Ona Munson, who had performed brilliantly in a screen test.

The casting of the principal African-American roles was almost automatic: The part of Scarlett's mammy went to Hattie McDaniel, a talented actress who had made a career out of playing jolly, sympathetic maids in Hollywood films. The role of Prissy went with similar ease to

Butterfly McQueen, whose squeaky voice and twitchy mannerisms had made her a comedic fixture on the stage as well as in films.

Ann Rutherford stepped out of her role as Mickey Rooney's friend in the Andy Hardy films to play Scarlett O'Hara's older sister. And, wondrously, a number of the young women imported from the hinterlands of Georgia during the great Scarlett search—through either sheer good luck or sexual compliance—wound up actually playing minor roles in the film. For most of them, it was the start and the end of their movie careers.

TURNING THE NOVEL INTO A SCRIPT

All this time, the task of turning Margaret Mitchell's sprawling novel into a makeable movie had been in the hands of screenwriter Sidney Howard. It was no simple task. Story editors originally estimated that if *Gone with the Wind* were translated fully and completely into a movie, the film would last 117 hours. But Selznick was confident that Howard could do the job. He was already a Pulitzer Prize-winning playwright and a highly respected hand at turning out award-winning scripts.

After working for over three months at both his Los Angeles and New York apartments, Howard delivered a script just under four hundred pages in length. It made Selznick restless, both because he had not himself fully participated in its creation and because his production people estimated it would result in a movie lasting about six hours. Selznick briefly considered turning the novel into two movies, to be released consecutively. Instead, he decided to call in new writers.

A veritable parade of scripters was put on the project by Selznick, including veterans Oliver Garrett, John Van Druten, Jo Swerling, and even the famed novelist F. Scott Fitzgerald. Selznick schooled all of them in his belief that the central story of a novel should be preserved without significant change, but that whole chunks of action could be left out as long as the script was faithful to certain scenes and dialogue that readers would be likely to remember.

Eventually, a workable shooting script began to emerge, but Selznick still regarded it as a work-in-progress. The script continued to be altered and shifted even after shooting began. The fluidity of the script took its toll on the directing staff and actors alike. Frequently, new pages would arrive the day before, or even the morning of, shooting. The "mother script," kept by Selznick himself, became a rainbow of colors, as pages color-coded to identify the various writers and the dates of change were constantly inserted and withdrawn.

Sidney Howard

THE FILMING GETS UNDER WAY

Actual filming got under way in January of 1939. Selznick anticipated a smooth-running production, but during the first days of shooting, it became obvious that there were problems. Early scenes seemed slow and overly labored to Selznick. Director George Cukor's preoccupation with getting meaningful performances out of Leigh and de Havilland was slowing down the action. Cukor was giving Selznick character development when what Selznick wanted was melodrama. Moreover, Gable was not happy. He felt Cukor was favoring his female leads and leaving Gable's character to fend for itself. Gable was a megastar and he was accustomed to being treated like one. The net of it was that, with almost no notice, Selznick fired Cukor from the film and replaced him with Victor Fleming, a longtime buddy and cohort of Gable.

A NEW DIRECTOR—A NEW PROBLEM

Victor Fleming came to the film with impressive credentials. He began his Hollywood career as a camera assistant, a cinematographer, and an assistant director. He came into his own as a director of silent films starring such notables as Douglas Fairbanks. In the early thirties, he achieved fame as the director of some of MGM's most successful films, including *Red Dust*, *Treasure Island*, and *Captains Courageous*. Fleming was known as a "man's director" and had already directed Gable in several films. Remarkably, Fleming was hauled off the set of *The Wizard of Oz*, scarcely a "man's film," to take up the task of directing *Gone with the Wind*.

Victor Fleming

One of the first things Fleming did was to march into Selznick's office and announce: "The problem with this fucking movie is that it's got no fucking script!"

With that pronouncement, Selznick decided to call a halt to filming until an acceptable final script could be hammered out. To perform that miracle, Selznick decided to call on Ben Hecht. Hecht had a reputation as a brilliant movie script craftsman. A native New Yorker, Hecht had authored a number of successful films, including *Front Page*, for which he had received an Academy Award. Hecht was summoned to Hollywood to see what he could do. When Hecht arrived for his preliminary meeting on the rewrite, Selznick was astonished to discover that he had never read the book—and, moreover, he didn't plan to read it. Selznick, with the film hanging in the balance, made a dramatic decision: He would lock himself, along with Hecht and Fleming, in his office until a final script was finished. To accomplish this, he imported several typewriters, lined up a succession of secretaries, and stocked the office with peanuts and bananas—foods that he believed activated the mind and stimulated the creative juices. As an added precaution, he laid in a supply of benzedrine tablets.

The lockup lasted almost a week, with none of the participants daring to leave. Too much was at stake. One early discovery in the session was that Fleming had also not read the book. With Hecht at the typewriter, Selznick recited the story line while he and Fleming then acted out the various roles. Selznick specialized in Scarlett and Melanie, Fleming in Rhett and Ashley. There were arguments and physical collapses (Fleming began bleeding from one eye). But somehow they kept going and, when the door was finally opened, they had a decent, if not polished, shooting script.

THE MOVIE SCRIPT FOR
GONE WITH THE WIND, PART ONE

It is spring of 1861 in pre-Civil War Georgia. Scarlett O'Hara is a pretty, fiery, young Southern belle, daughter of Gerald O'Hara, a wealthy Irish immigrant, and Ellen O'Hara, who is of French ancestry. At their plantation home called Tara, Scarlett is seen flirting with the Tarleton brothers on the front lawn of a garden party. The twins reveal to Scarlett that her secret love, Ashley Wilkes, is to be married to his cousin, Melanie Hamilton. Scarlett learns that the engagement will be announced the following day at Twelve Oaks, Ashley's neighboring plantation. There is talk of a coming war with the North.

At Twelve Oaks, Scarlett finds herself being admired by a newcomer, Rhett Butler. She learns that Butler is an expellee from West Point and a gambler. Butler proceeds to make himself unpopular by proclaiming that the South cannot possibly win a war against the North. Scarlett, instead of taking her regular afternoon siesta, sneaks into Ashley's library where she confesses that she has always loved him. Ashley proclaims his love in return but says he thinks Melanie will make a more compatible wife. Scarlett, feeling betrayed, slaps Ashley, who then leaves. Butler, who has been sleeping unseen on a couch, tells Scarlett that he overheard the entire encounter and that he will keep her secret. Outside, the party is interrupted by young men arriving on horseback to announce that war has broken out. The men rush off to enlist. Later, Scarlett watches Ashley kissing Melanie and realizes her love for him is fruitless. Still later, Melanie's younger brother, Charles Hamilton, proposes marriage to Scarlett. In a spirit of revenge, she accepts and they are married just before her new husband leaves for the war.

Scarlett's marriage is short lived, as Charles dies while serving in the Confederate army from pneumonia and measles. Scarlett's mother suggests that she recover from her loss by visiting the Hamilton home in Atlanta. Scarlett's housemaid, Mammy, warns her that she should not go for the purpose of waiting for Ashley to return from the war. Scarlett decamps for Atlanta.

SELZNICK INTERNATIONAL

presents

"GONE WITH THE WIND"

from the novel by

MARGARET MITCHELL

starring

CLARK GABLE

VIVIEN LEIGH

LESLIE HOWARD

OLIVIA DE HAVILLAND

Final Shooting Script
January 24, 1939

Screenplay by Sidney Howard

Produced by David O. Selznick

Directed by Victor Fleming

The shooting script for *Gone with the Wind*, signed by the cast

Instead of acting the bereaved widow, Scarlett attends a charity ball with Melanie. Her appearance as a widow in search of fun shocks the assembled, and she shocks them again by accepting a one-hundred-dollar bid at the dance auction from Butler, who has returned as a Confederate hero because of his blockade-running activity. As they dance, he tells her of his determination to become her lover. Scarlett scoffs and proclaims that will never happen.

With the defeat at Gettysburg, the tide of war turns against the Confederacy. Sherman's army rampages through the South and leaves Atlanta a scene of death and destruction. In the midst of the chaos, Melanie, in the company of Scarlett, goes into labor. Scarlett remembers her pledge to Ashley to take care of Melanie. She and her young house servant, Prissy, are forced to assist in the delivery without medical assistance. Despite Prissy's inability to help ("I don't know nuthin' about birthin"), Scarlett succeeds in saving the baby and the mother. Desperate for help, she later pleads with Butler to help them to go to Tara. He appears with a horse and wagon, saves them, and together they ride through a burned-out and flaming Atlanta and head for Scarlett's ancestral home. Then Rhett, realizing his greater duty is to the Confederacy, leaves Scarlett, Melanie, Prissy, and the baby to fend for themselves. On their way to Tara, the group passes Twelve Oaks, which is now deserted, burned out, and ruined. When she finally arrives at Tara, Scarlett is relieved to find it still standing, but now deserted except for her father, her sister, and two servants. She learns that her mother has died of typhoid fever and that her father has lost his mind from grief. Tara has been pillaged by Union troops and the once prosperous farmlands have been destroyed. Scarlett dramatically vows, with her hands raised to the heavens, that she will overcome everything and survive ("As God is my witness, I will never be hungry again!").

(INTERMISSION)

The iconic image from *Gone with the Wind*

Part Two

Scarlett determines to restore Tara as a productive plantation, but troubles mount. A Union soldier invades the premises, burglarizes Tara, and threatens Scarlett. She seizes a gun and kills him. Eventually, Ashley returns and confesses his continuing love for Scarlett, but says he cannot leave the faithful Melanie. He tries to help in the salvaging of Tara, but his efforts are ineffective. Scarlett's demented father dies after he falls from a runaway horse.

A desperate Scarlett decides to try to capture the affections—and the wealth—of Rhett Butler, who has returned to Atlanta. When she finally locates Butler, he is in jail and he lets her know that his bank accounts have all been blocked because of his war activities. As she leaves the jailhouse, she encounters her sister's fiancé, the middle-aged Frank Kennedy. When she learns that Kennedy has become a prosperous entrepreneur, she decides to set her own cap for Kennedy, telling him, untruthfully, that her sister has wearied of waiting for him and has married someone else. Scarlett then marries Frank and manages to take over his affairs and becomes a rich woman in her own right. One of her properties is a mill, and, in a final effort to reconnect with Ashley, she implores him to help her run the enterprise. Melanie consents to this new arrangement, but Ashley once again proves to be an ineffective manager. However, when Scarlett is set upon one day by Northern scalawags, Ashley and others make a retributive attack on the shantytown where the outliers live. In the battle that ensues, Ashley is wounded and Frank is killed.

Shortly after Frank's funeral, Scarlett reunites with Rhett Butler and, realizing that Butler is once again a wealthy man, she agrees to marry him. Rhett, fully aware of Scarlett's motives, takes her to New Orleans on a honeymoon trip, pledging to win her love. Rhett then decides to restore Tara to its former glory, but Scarlett goes off on her own and, using Rhett's money, builds herself the largest mansion in Atlanta. Scarlett becomes pregnant and has a daughter.

Butler devotes all his love to his daughter, Bonnie Blue, and does his best to restore his own reputation with Atlanta society for her sake. Scarlett lets Rhett know that she does not want any more children and she locks the door that separates their bedrooms. Rhett does not accept her denial of love and kicks open the door. Later, he has the door removed entirely.

One day at the mill, Scarlett and Ashley talk of things past. Ashley relates the story of his own sad life, and Scarlett, out of sympathy and understanding, embraces him. The encounter is witnessed by two ladies who spread rumors about Scarlett and Ashley that further tarnish Scarlett's reputation in Atlanta.

Rhett, having heard the rumors of Scarlett's faithlessness, forces her out of bed that night and makes her attend a birthday party for Ashley. Later that night, Scarlett arrives home to find Rhett drunk and enraged. He tells her that he will kill her if it is the only way to make her forget Ashley. He then carries her upstairs, declaring, "This is one night you're not turning me out!"

Scarlett's maid,
portrayed by Hattie
McDaniel, informs
Scarlett of her
expanding waistline.

Rhett returns later the next day to apologize for his brutish behavior and he offers to divorce her. Scarlett refuses the offer, fearing that a divorce would only add to her already unsavory reputation. Rhett then decides he needs to remove his beloved Bonnie Blue from the unhappy environs of Atlanta and he takes her to London on an extended vacation. But when Bonnie experiences nightmares, he concludes that she needs her mother's love as well as his own. Rhett returns and Scarlett is happy to see him and informs him that she is again pregnant. An argument ensues and, when Scarlett lunges at Rhett in a rage, she slips and falls down the stairs. As a result of the fall Scarlett suffers a miscarriage.

After Scarlett recovers from her miscarriage, Bonnie Blue is tragically killed when she attempts to jump a fence while riding a pony her father has given her. Scarlett blames Rhett for her death, and Rhett is so devastated that he locks himself in a room with his daughter's body, refusing to surrender it for a funeral. Melanie arrives to comfort both Scarlett and Rhett, but then collapses because of problems with a second pregnancy that she was told could kill her. As Melanie lies dying, she extracts a pledge from Scarlett that she will look after Ashley and that she will return to Rhett, who truly loves her. When Melanie dies, Ashley collapses in grief, proving to Scarlett that he really did love Melanie all along.

Scarlett rushes home to rescue her marriage to Rhett, only to find him packing to leave. Scarlett pleads with him to stay, saying that she now realizes that she never really loved Ashley and that it was Rhett she loved all along. Rhett refuses her entreaties and tells her that, with Bonnie Blue dead, there is nothing to hold their marriage together. As he leaves, Scarlett wails in misery: "Rhett. If you go, where shall I go? What shall I do?" Rhett makes his final pronouncement: "Frankly, my dear, I don't give a damn." He then walks away into the morning fog.

Scarlett, sitting on the stairs, weeps copiously and then hears a succession of voices—Rhett, Gerald, Ashley—all of whom remind her that her true soul and real strength reside at Tara. As she brightens, Scarlett blurts: "Tara! Home! I'll go home and find a way to get him back! After all, tomorrow is another day!"

Scarlett returns to Tara and once again stands before the decaying mansion, resolute and unconquerable.

THE END

The script made a number of changes to Mitchell's novel, most of them minor. Scarlett's first two children were nowhere to be found. The Tarleton twins, Scarlett's original suitors, were now the Tarleton brothers. Rhett's long and confessional description of his illegal blockade activities was out. The Ku Klux Klan, which occupied some considerable space in the novel, was never mentioned. In a bow to the Hayes Office, Belle Walting, Rhett's prostitute friend, was transformed into a sort of congenial hostess. Most of the steamy love scenes were either eliminated or toned down, once again in deference to the Hayes Office. A number of Mitchell's minor characters failed to make an appearance. Still, the essence of Mitchell's work ran throughout the script, and the basic plot structure and the important characters remained. Of equal importance, Selznick had seen to it that the most memorable quotes and dialogues remained.

TROUBLE ON THE SET

Production had been halted for seventeen days to get the script into shape, and now there was a sense of urgency to get the film shot. Gable arrived on set the first day, happily showing off his "penis warmer" that paramour Carole Lombard had knitted for him. After just a few days on the set, trouble was already brewing.

Despite many light moments on the set, the relationship between Leigh and Gable was frequently contentious. The actress was often frustrated with Gable's inability to be ready when shooting was scheduled to begin. Gable was frequently in his dressing room, memorizing his lines. Often Leigh would yell out in frustration, "Why are we fucking about!" Gable had trouble creating a Southern accent and was constantly working off to the side with Susan Myrick, his voice coach.

There was also a revealing difference in the attitude that Leigh and Gable had toward the novel itself. Leigh's was almost reverential; she carried a copy of the book to the set, constantly read from it during shooting breaks, and seemed to use it as a source of inspiration and strength. On the other hand, Gable would boast, through the remainder of his life, that he never read the book. Leigh also complained before each kissing scene that she found Gable's breath offensive.

Leigh also irritated Gable with her talent and professionalism. While Gable struggled with his lines and his accent, Leigh could turn it on and off like a faucet. One second she would be telling the cameramen a raunchy British joke, and the next second she would be doing Scarlett O'Hara to perfection. Also, there was a difference between the two in their work ethic: Gable never seemed in any hurry and insisted on leaving the set promptly at 6:00 P.M., while Leigh was constantly pushing to get the film completed.

Scarlett and Rhett

Among other things, she was anxious to reunite with Laurence Olivier, who was on the stage in New York. After one of their too-infrequent weekend reunions in Los Angeles, Leigh gleefully reported to Gable, "We just fucked and fucked and fucked!"

There was also a sense of strain on the set. Victor Fleming was irritated by the fact that Leigh was getting private instruction on her scenes from the previous director, George Cukor. Finally, there was a blowup on the set. When Leigh complained about her lines in the script for the umpteenth time, Fleming yelled, "Miss Leigh, you can stick this script up your royal ass!" and stormed off the set. Only the combined apologies and entreaties of both Leigh and Gable convinced him to return.

Selznick had now made his decision that *Gone with the Wind* would be a single movie, despite its length, but that the film would be divided into two parts. Filming continued at a frenzied pace. Gable was having so much trouble speaking like a Southerner that a decision was made to just "let Gable be Gable." As for Leigh, she seemed to become more demanding and, at the same time, more fragile as filming continued. She constantly complained about the script and especially about her lines, many of which she felt were stilted or out of character. Still, she soldiered on, giving remarkable performances day after day. Her growing emotional state was probably a precursor of her later mental problems.

PRODUCTION PUSHES AHEAD

Almost all of the scenes were shot on stage sets in the Selznick studios. Tara itself was a mock-up of the front of the plantation mansion superimposed on the filmed scenes in a process called "matte painting." Because the film was being shot in the new process called "Technicolor," experts from the company that owned the process were always on hand, advising on color and lighting.

All in all, *Gone with the Wind* required the creation of thousands of costumes, from drab military uniforms to Scarlett's spectacular dresses. As for Gable's outfits, they were handsewn for him by his own personal tailor after the designs given him by the studio. Selznick was obsessed with the appropriateness of the costumes in every scene. Knowing

Gable and Leigh in a lighter moment on the set

that Scarlett would be appearing in the same calico print dress over an extended period of time, he had the dress made in twenty-seven different stages of deterioration, with Leigh continuously redressing to reflect the passage of time and the decline of her fortunes.

In the scene when Scarlett searches for a doctor in the Atlanta railway depot, more than 1,500 wounded and dying Confederate soldiers are seen lying on the ground. When the scene was over and the director yelled "Cut!," only half of the soldiers arose. The rest remained on the ground. They were dummies dressed in Confederate uniforms.

A hundred and fifty days had passed between the filming of the burning of Atlanta on December 10, 1938, and a final reshoot of the opening scene on July 1, 1939. Gable's final line is perhaps the most recognizable single line in movie history. In Mitchell's book, Rhett says simply, "My dear, I don't give a damn." The addition of the word "Frankly" turned it into movie history. At least three of the writers involved in the script would later take credit for the insertion of the magical word.

Filming of the Atlanta railway depot scenes

WRAPPING IT UP

While *Gone with the Wind* was finally "in the can," that didn't mean the problems were over. After its first cut, the movie ran almost five hours, an intolerable length for a film, even though it was divided into two parts with an intermission.

Selznick personally supervised the editing of the film, cutting out what he felt were precious and vital scenes, but realizing full well that theater operators would object to any film of that length. Max Steiner, a veteran composer of music for such films as *Jezebel*, *A Star Is Born*, and *King Kong*, was selected to write the score for the film. Working around the clock, Steiner came up with more than three hours of music, including an overarching theme and tonal music for the various principal characters. Eventually, Selznick managed to edit his masterpiece down to four hours and twenty minutes for the presentation at the traditional prescreening before a live audience.

That screening took place in the Warner Theater in Santa Barbara. The audience jumped to its feet and applauded the moment the opening title came on the screen. They sat enthralled through the showing, demonstrating emotion and enthusiasm. At the end, the audience sat for a moment in stunned silence. They had never seen anything like it. They rose again and cheered. The audience review cards were uniformly ecstatic. Selznick, on the way home in his car, wept with joy.

There was more to be done. The film was still too long for release. Agonizingly, Selznick and his crew carved out another fifty-six minutes. A number of brilliantly filmed and acted scenes wound up on the cutting room floor.

Now that the filming was complete, the Hayes Office needed to be dealt with. It is difficult today to imagine the power and the prudery of this censorious body. It had come into being in response to what was said to be a declining morality in films. Wilbur Hayes, a stern-faced former postmaster of the United States, was selected to become a sort of czar over the appropriateness of what was shown in American films. His office eventually came up with a set of rules and standards that today seem ludicrous. An actor and actress could not be shown in bed together, even if they were portraying a married couple. Women could not show any part of the leg unless they were dancing. Kisses could not last more than seventeen frames of film. Only villains and seductresses could smoke cigarettes.

Selznick and his writers had scrupulously scrubbed scenes from the book that would show sexual heat. Language was refined so that soldiers never cursed, and the word "nigger," used frequently in the book, never found its way into the script. But now, after filming was completed, Selznick encountered a problem he had not foreseen.

Rhett's final line in the book included the word "damn," and it was, he was sure, a line every reader would remember. The Hayes Office banned profanity of all kinds. Not only was "damn" considered a curse word by the Hayes Office, but it also fell into their category of "four-letter words." Selznick was certain that if Rhett didn't say "Frankly, my

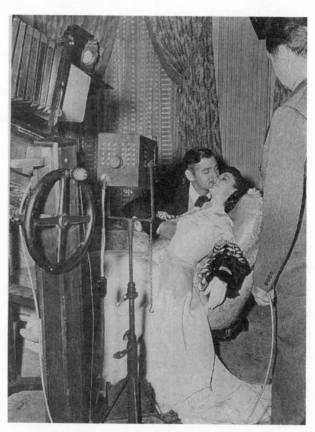

Fleming filming Gable and Leigh

dear, I don't give a damn!" lovers of the book would be disappointed and the film's finale would be damaged. He put on a full campaign to permit the use of the word, pointing out to Hayes himself that the *Oxford English Dictionary* defined the word, not as an oath, but as a vulgarism. Hayes, an admirer of the novel, finally gave Selznick a waiver. The immortal line was preserved in celluloid, but Hayes, in order to preserve his own integrity, fined Selznick for a technical violation.

Wilbur Hayes

When accountants at Selznick Studios finally rang up the total of all the costs in making *Gone with the Wind*, the amount came to $3,957,000. It was more money than anyone had ever spent to produce a motion picture. To earn its way into a profit, the film would require a massive publicity campaign and a movie premiere like no other.

THE MOVIE TAKES ATLANTA

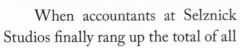

The decision was made to premiere *Gone with the Wind* in Atlanta on December 15, 1939, and to open up all the spigots. The event had the feel of both a grand national event and a triumphal military parade. Over three days, *Gone with the Wind* conquered Atlanta almost as thoroughly as Sherman had some seventy-five years earlier. The governor of Georgia declared the event a statewide holiday. When the stars arrived, they were greeted like gods from another planet. When Gable stepped out of his own private plane, hundreds of fans made a mad rush for "Rhett." The members of the band hired to greet him with a rendition of "Dixie" had to flee for their lives. The parade into town featured open cars packed with the actors, accompanied by local dignitaries dressed in period costumes. Peachtree Street was lined with fans and sightseers, six and seven deep at the curbside.

1939

Cutting the film of *Gone with the Wind*

Over the next several days, there were press conferences, receptions, and a grand ball. At one of these events, Clark Gable and Margaret Mitchell met for the first time. As they chatted, a crowd pressed around them trying to overhear their conversation. Mitchell solved the problem by taking Clark Gable by the hand and leading him into the Ladies' Room, locking the door behind them. History does not record what they talked about.

The movie premiered at Atlanta's Grand Theatre. The 1,400 invitees cheered and applauded throughout the showing. One of the biggest cheers came when war with the North was announced on the screen. Afterward, the all-white audience wildly applauded the actors themselves, seemingly unaware that none of the black actors were present.

The film opened nationally to great acclaim. By Christmas, ticket sales had already passed the one-million-dollar mark. Critics fell all over themselves praising the film. *The New York Times* called it "the greatest motion picture mural we have ever seen and the most spectacular film-making adventure in Hollywood's spectacular history." Even cynics fell under its spell. Critic Frank Nugent penned, "It has arrived at last, and we cannot get over the shock of not being disappointed." *Variety* took a more practical, but equally enthusiastic, view, saying, "*Gone with the Wind* is poised for grosses that may be second to none in the history of the business." They were right. In its initial release, Metro priced tickets at $1.00 and $1.50 for evening performances, seventy-five cents for morning and afternoon showings. One year after it opened, more than twenty-five million people had seen the movie.

The Sweep

Gone with the Wind was nominated for thirteen Academy Awards. The ceremony was held at the Cocoanut Grove in the Ambassador Hotel in Los Angeles. When the nominations had all been read, the winners announced, and the speeches made, *Gone with the Wind*, had garnered an astonishing ten Oscars. Vivien Leigh was named Best Actress; Victor Fleming, Best Director; Hattie McDaniel, Best Supporting Actress; Sidney Howard, Best Screenwriter. The film also won awards for Best Art Direction, Best Special Effects, Best Editing, Best Photography, and Best Use of Color Film. Selznick himself was given a special Oscar for film achievement.

However, not everyone involved with the film came away a winner. Clark Gable lost to Robert Donat, who won for his role in *Goodbye, Mr. Chips*. Gable was not a cheerful loser and felt that his performance as Rhett Butler had been unfairly overshadowed by Leigh's Scarlett O'Hara. At the dinner that followed the awards, his wife, Carole Lombard, said, "We shouldn't be too disappointed. There'll be other chances to win." Gable replied that he didn't think so, that his best chance had been the Butler role. Replied Lombard, "Not you, you self-centered bastard. I meant me!"

After Gone with the Wind

Clark Gable lost his wife, Carole Lombard, just two years after the release of *Gone with the Wind*. She has just completed her thirty-seventh film and was on her way home from a war bond appearance when the plane she was on crashed into a mountain near Las Vegas. It was a tragedy from which Gable never fully recovered. With the advent of World War II, he enlisted in the Army Air Corp and spent most of the war in England with the 351st Bomber Group. He supervised training films to promote aerial gunnery, a skill in which he had received extensive training. He flew a number of combat missions, including one in which he narrowly escaped death. Before the end of the war, he rose to the rank of major, and, at the end of the war, his discharge papers were signed by Captain Ronald Reagan. Gable was awarded the Air Medal and the Distinguished Flying Cross. Papers later found in Germany revealed that Gable was Hitler's favorite actor and that he had offered an enormous reward to any German soldier who could capture him alive.

Following the war, Gable resumed his film career, starring in twenty-three more films, including *The Hucksters*, *Command Decision*, *Mogambo*, *Soldier of Fortune*, *Band of Angels*, *Teacher's Pet*, and *But*

Carole Lombard and Clark Gable, Hollywood's golden couple

Gone with the Wind **opens to the public.**

Not for Me. His final film was *The Misfits,* in which he costarred with Marilyn Monroe. Gable married two more times and fathered a child, a daughter, with actress Loretta Young. He died in 1960 at the age of 59 after suffering a heart attack. Because MGM had refused to renew his contract in 1953, Gable became embittered toward his old studio. When they held a lavish party to celebrate the twentieth anniversary of *Gone with the Wind,* Gable refused to attend.

✻ ✻ ✻

Vivien Leigh never basked in her celebrity as the Academy Award-winning actress of *Gone with the Wind.* In fact, she refused to consider herself a film star. Her first love was the stage and she was eager to resume her earlier career in the theater. After the Academy Award ceremony, she and her husband, Laurence Olivier, mounted a successful stage production of *Romeo and Juliet* on Broadway. The demand for their continued services in Hollywood enticed them to costar in *That Hamilton Woman,* a film that was admired by President Roosevelt and Winston Churchill, and both war leaders entertained the famous acting couple numerous times. In 1943, Leigh traveled extensively, entertaining British troops, but eventually fell ill from the strain. She was later diagnosed with tuberculosis, a disease from which she never completely recovered. Leigh also began having fits of depression and was eventually deemed to be bipolar. After the war, however, her acting career continued to thrive. She and Olivier traveled the world, staging plays, both classic and contemporary, usually to critical acclaim and adoring audiences. In 1947, Olivier was knighted by the queen at Buckingham Palace. Leigh automatically became Lady Olivier, a title she did not hesitate to employ.

Leigh won rave reviews during her London performance in Tennessee Williams' *A Streetcar Named Desire* and later played the role of Blanche DuBois in the Hollywood film version. For that performance, she won her second Academy Award, as well as the British Academy Award as film actress of the year. Despite her mental instability and a traumatic divorce from Olivier, Leigh continued to do outstanding work in films such as *The Roman Spring of Mrs. Stone* and *Ship of Fools.* Eventually, her tuberculosis returned and her health failed. She died in July of 1967, with Olivier at her bedside. Said author and critic Garson Kanin, "Vivien Leigh was a stunner whose ravishing beauty often tended

Selznick and Leigh at the Academy Awards

to obscure her staggering achievements as an actress. Great beauties are seldom great actresses—simply because they don't have to be. Vivien was the exception. She was ambitious, persevering, serious, often inspiring."

❋ ❋ ❋

Olivia de Havilland continued to make films for Warner Brothers following her award-winning performance as Melanie, but she became increasingly disenchanted with the roles offered her by the studio. Warner suspended her in 1940 but refused to release her from her contract. She sued the filmmaker and won a court decision that changed Hollywood forever. After what became known as "The de Havilland Law," studios were no longer able to "own" stars for an indefinite period of time. Though Warner banned de Havilland from its lots, she went on to continue a successful career in films, starring in *Devotion*, *The Dark Mirror*, *To Each His Own*, and *The Heiress*. She was once again nominated for an Academy Award for *The Snake Pit*, in which she played a woman with serious mental illness. She continued making movies well into the 1960s, performing in such films as *Lady in a Cage*, *Noon Wine*, and television movie *Anastasia*. De Havilland eventually retired from films and moved to Paris with her husband, French journalist Pierre Galante. She outlived all the other principal actors who appeared in *Gone with the Wind*.

❋ ❋ ❋

Hattie McDaniel, celebrated as the first black actress to win an Academy Award, continued to work in motion pictures and in radio. She performed in a number of Warner Brothers films during the 1940s and 1950s, including *In This Our Life* with Bette Davis and *Thank Your Lucky Stars* with Humphrey Bogart. She was also active in radio and television, and she became the first African American to star in her own show, the comedy series *Beulah*. She died in 1952 of breast cancer. When criticized for playing so many roles as a maid, McDaniel once replied, "Why should I complain about making $700 a week playing a maid? If I didn't, I'd be making $7 a week being one."

✳ ✳ ✳

Leslie Howard, who had reluctantly taken on the role of Ashley Wilkes, is best remembered for his fine performance in the role. After the film's release, Howard returned to his native England. He starred in a number of British war films, including *49th Parallel*, *Pimpernel Smith*, and *The First of the Few*. Howard died in 1943 on a flight from England to Portugal when a Junker fighter shot his plane down in the mistaken belief that Winston Churchill was on board. Howard perished along with seventeen passengers and a crew of four. His body was never recovered.

✳ ✳ ✳

The author surrounded by the stars

In 1937, Margaret Mitchell won the Pulitzer Prize for her novel. She spent the next decade in quiet celebrity, living in her home and community in Atlanta, Georgia. In 1949, just ten years after the publication of *Gone with the Wind*, she was killed by a drunken driver as she stepped off the curb on Peachtree Street, the site of the elaborate parade that had heralded the opening of her film. Over time, her novel was translated into more than fifty languages and sold more than fifty million copies. She never published another book.

✳ ✳ ✳

David O. Selznick continued producing motion pictures for the next twenty years. His successful films included *Spellbound*, *The Paradine Case*, *Since You Went Away*, *The Third Man*, *Duel in the Sun*, and *A Farewell to Arms*. He was nominated for the Academy Award seven times and won again for *Rebecca*. He died in 1965 after several heart attacks. Just five years after making *Gone with the Wind*, Selznick sold all the rights to the film to MGM, not realizing the potential profits it could yield in rereleases in television and DVD sales.

✻ ✻ ✻

On its initial run alone, *Gone with the Wind* established itself as the number one money-making film in history. By the middle of 1943, it had grossed $32 million just in the United States, and its popularity overseas, even during wartime, flooded the Metro coffers with additional millions. By the mid-1960s, total revenues had swelled to $75 million. In today's dollars, that total would outstrip any other film shown over a similar period of time. And *Gone with the Wind* continues to generate additional revenue in release after release. It is generally conceded that *Gone with the Wind* has been seen by more people than any other movie ever made. To date, more than 202 million people have paid at the box office to see *Gone with the Wind*—24 million more than *Star Wars*, its nearest competitor. In 1977, the Association of Motion Picture Directors officially cited *Gone with the Wind* as "The Greatest Movie Ever Made."

Poster for *Gone with the Wind*

GONE WITH THE WIND
THE FINAL FACTS

Studio:	Metro-Goldwyn-Mayer
Executive Producer:	David O. Selznick
Director:	Victor Fleming
Screenplay:	Sidney Howard
Original Story:	Margaret Mitchell
Cinematography:	Ernest Haller and Ray Rennaham
Art Direction:	Lyle Wheeler
Release Date:	December 15, 1939
Running Time:	222 minutes
Cost of Production:	$3,850,000
Box Office (original three-year run):	$34,000,000 (est.)
Total Worldwide Box Office to date:	$400,175,000 (est.)

Cast

Rhett Butler .... Clark Gable
Scarlett O'Hara .... Vivien Leigh
Ashley Wilkes.. Leslie Howard
Melanie Hamilton .... Olivia de Havilland
Gerald O'Hara....................................... Thomas Mitchell
Mammy .... Hattie McDaniel
Prissy .... Butterfly McQueen
Suellen O'Hara .... Evelyn Keyes
Ellen O'Hara.. Barbara O'Neil
Frank Kennedy .... Carroll Nye
Charles Hamilton .... Rand Brooks
Belle Watling.. Ona Munson
Bonnie Blue Butler .... Cammie King

Awards

Academy Awards Won: David O Selznick for Best Picture; Victor
Fleming for Best Director; Vivien Leigh for Best Actress; Hattie
McDaniel for Best Actress in a Supporting Role; Best Art Direction;
Best Color Cinematography; Best Film Editing; Best Screenplay; Best
Special Effects; Best Original Music; Best Sound Recording.

Collier's Magazine

STAGECOACH

THE STORY

It was a rainy morning in Portland, Oregon, and Erny Haycox was walking the two miles from his home to his writing office on Sandy Boulevard on the eastern side of town. It was a walk he made every weekday and he always enjoyed the stroll, not just for the exercise but also because it cleared his head for the morning's work. But this morning he was somewhat concerned because he carried with him a letter that had arrived in yesterday's afternoon mail that posed a challenge.

After he arrived at his office, he took a brief moment to say hello to the lawyer who shared the adjoining office, noted that his secretary was not in, opened a window to clear the air of yesterday's cigar smoke, and sat down at the plain table that served as his writing desk. He took out the letter and read it again. Usually, requests for his work came through his New York agent, but this had come directly from Ken Littauer, the editor of *Collier's* magazine. Littauer was requesting a Western story of some three thousand words for publication in the issue of May 10, 1937. Haycox was flattered because *Collier's* had become his principal source of income and it paid well. In the unwritten agreement he had with the magazine, Haycox received $10,000 for a serialized story of ten or more installments and $800 for a short story. It was important to keep up the relationship and to accommodate *Collier's* whenever he could.

As the request had come directly from the editor, Haycox felt a special need to deliver. The problem was that the May issue had a lead

Haycox writing at his desk

time of at least six weeks. It was already the middle of February and he didn't yet have a story to tell.

Deadlines were not usually a serious problem for Haycox. For him, the secret of creation was application. He had a low regard for writers who waited for the muse to strike. He didn't believe in writer's block. The way to write was to write—and to keep on writing. He took out a piece of paper, placed it in the roller of his Remington typewriter, and began to type. He knew *Collier's* wanted a story of the early West, involving cowboys and Indians, because whenever one of his Western stories appeared, the magazine's circulation jumped as much as fifty thousand readers. The first task was to set the mood, and so he began to type.

> *This was one of those years in the Territory when*
> *Apache smoke signals spiraled up from the stony mountain*
> *summits and many a ranch cabin lay*
> *as a square of blackened ashes on the ground.*

He leaned back and lit up a cigar. It was a good start. The rest was sure to come. It always had.

For more than fifteen years, Haycox had been turning out readable, sometimes inspired, prose. As a student at the University of Oregon, he took over a cookhouse at his fraternity, turned it into a writing den, and, with no experience as an author, began typing out stories and submitting them to small publications. After two years, his den was papered with rejection slips. Believing that perspiration was more important than inspiration, he kept diligently at his typewriter, sometimes far into the night. He wrote stories with all kinds of plots and characters—sea stories, Westerns, urban tales, histories, and thrillers. Finally, in 1923, his diligence began to pay off. His first acceptance was for a story about a young soldier on the Mexican border, and he got a check for $30 from one of the pulp magazines. Soon other stories went out from the den and other checks floated in.

He left college after two years, deciding to be a full-time writer living in the real world. He worked as a newspaper reporter, he kept writing, and he kept selling stories. He moved to New York, where, for a brief time, he wrote reviews and serialized novels. He got married, hired an agent, and spent every extra dollar he had on books. He returned to Oregon and, over the ensuing years, built a reputation as a solid family man—and as a dependable and successful author. By 1937, he had published more than a hundred stories and novellas as well as a half-dozen full-length novels. He also became something of a local Portland celebrity and a well-known figure in the literary world.

Despite his growing fame and success, his main source of income was *Collier's* magazine. In fact, throughout the mid-1930s he wrote almost exclusively for *Collier's*, sending them his short stories and his serials, many of which were later converted into novels. His work was, with rare exceptions, always accepted for publication by fiction editor Littauer. That's why the reception of this letter from *Collier's* requesting a story for its spring issue demanded special attention.

Haycox as a young man

Haycox put down his cigar and began looking through his files. By now, he had been researching the history of the West for more than a decade, assembling his own personal library of books, drawings, photographs, newspaper clippings, and maps. He pulled out a chart of early stagecoach routes and studied it—and suddenly he remembered a legendary story by Guy de Maupassant called "Boule de Suif," in which a number of desperate passengers travel in a stagecoach. One of them is a prostitute, and during the journey the interplay between the passengers and their attitude

The Haycox Remington

toward the woman reveals their true characters. It was a great plot and there was no reason why a stagecoach traveling the early West couldn't also be used to create a great adventure venue. Haycox studied an early map of the Western territories for place names, as he regarded them as important parts of any story. They should have character and they should be authentic and convey a strong sense of place. He settled on the village of Tonto in Arizona as a starting point, and then, after some study, he added Lordsburg in southeastern New Mexico to his prospective scenario. The two villages were a little more than two hundred miles apart, a distance that a stage could cover easily in four or five days, about the right time for an action story. Haycox went back to his typewriter and, above the sentence he had written earlier, typed "Stage to Lordsburg." Then he added to his opening sentence: "... and the departure of a stage from Tonto was the beginning of an adventure that had no certain happy ending."

Haycox populated his stagecoach with a whore named Henriette and, for contrast, a pretty, upright girl journeying West to marry an army officer—then a whiskey drummer from St. Louis—then, again for contrast, a proper Englishman—and then, for Western authenticity, a cattleman and a gambler. Of course, he needed a hero. He settled on a somewhat mysterious blond cowboy he named "Malpais Bill" and gave him a personal mission of vengeance for his father's murder. Of course, the stage would travel through dangerous Apache territory.

From there on, Haycox's story proceeded at a gallop. The stage stopped at a place called Gap Creek and then at a town named Apache Wells. The characters played off on one another with shifting loyalties and surprising revelations. There was, of course, a romance between the blond cowboy and the lady of easy virtue—and there was a violent attack on the stagecoach by mounted Apache warriors. After the stage reached its destination, the cowboy hero triumphed in a gun battle with the evildoers, and there was a hint of life-ever-after between the two lovers. After typing for fourteen pages, Haycox put his final blessing on the story by cheerfully adding "The End."

The next morning, Erny Haycox did some polishing on his new story, put it in a manila envelope, walked to the post office, and mailed it to *Collier's* in New York. He was confident that he had given them a great story—and that he had gotten the manuscript to them in time.

John Ford Finds a Story

He was one of the busiest and most respected directors in Hollywood. He was John Ford—and his success had been hard won: He came to Hollywood in 1914, following his older brother, who was a movie writer and actor. He started out helping his brother in putting films together but soon branched out on his own. He learned his craft slowly but surely as an assistant and then, between 1917 and 1928, as a director on more than sixty silent shorts. His first major success was an ambitious historical drama called *The Iron Horse*, a dramatic account of the building of the Transcontinental Railroad. It was a true film epic, featuring thousands of extras, hundreds of Indians, two thousand horses, ten thousand cattle, the re-creation of two old trains, and the construction of two new towns. At the then breathtaking cost of $289,000, it grossed more than $2 million—and it put Ford in the front rank of Hollywood directors. From that point on, he was in such demand that it is difficult to keep track of all his pictures. On average, he made three films a year, films based on various themes and of varying quality. His subjects ranged from drama (*Napoleon's Barber*, in 1928) to adventure (*Riley the Cop*, in 1929) to comedy (*Men without Women*, in 1930). His film *Up the River* introduced two future stars to theater audiences: Spencer Tracy and Humphrey Bogart. Throughout the 1930s, his pictures improved in quality and in the degree of respect they commanded from the industry. *The Last Patrol*, in 1934, was named by the *New York Times* one of the top ten films of the year—and *The Informer*, in 1935, won Ford an Academy Award for Best Director. *Mary of Scotland*, in 1936, was not successful,

Ford, the aspiring director

but it starred Katharine Hepburn, and she won director Ford's heart. They commenced a celebrated love affair that became the talk of the industry.

Ford had been recognized early in his career as a master of the Western genre, but he had, in fact, not made a true Western film since 1926 (*3 Bad Men*). Despite his success with other subjects, he had a sentimental attachment to his early Westerns and the success they had brought him. As the end of the decade approached, Ford found himself keeping an eye out for a good Western tale.

Ford was now working for Columbia Studios and had surrounded himself with a team of top-notch collaborators, including scriptwriters Nunnally Johnson and Dudley Nichols. Early in 1937, they had brought him several Western stories that they thought had possibilities, but Ford rejected them for various reasons. Still, he was on the hunt.

In May of 1937, Ford picked up his new edition of *Collier's* and noted that a story by Ernest Haycox was marqueed on the cover. He was familiar with Haycox's work and had heard that Cecil B. DeMille was in the process of purchasing one of his stories. He opened the magazine and began reading "Stage to Lordsburg." By the time he finished reading, he was certain he had found his new Western.

Ford asked his business partner, Merian Cooper, to negotiate for the film rights. Within days, a deal was made, and Ford announced to the industry that he had purchased the rights to "Stage to Lordsburg" for $4,000. This was in the best tradition of Hollywood hyperbole. In

By Ernest Haycox

Where life ended for some, and began for others. The cleaning of the slate by the man known as Malpais Bill, and some new and more enduring writing upon it by the same gentleman

ILLUSTRATED BY
RONALD McLEOD

STAGE TO LORDSBURG

THIS was one of those years in the Territory when Apache smoke signals spiraled up from the stony mountain summits and many a ranch house lay as a square of blackened ashes on the ground and the departure of a stage from Tonto was the beginning of an adventure that had no certain happy ending. . . .

The stage and its six horses waited in front of Weilner's store on the north side of Tonto's square. Happy Stuart was on the box, the ribbons between his fingers and one foot teetering on the brake; and John Strang rode shotgun guard, and an escort of ten cavalrymen waited behind the coach, half asleep in their saddles.

At four-thirty in the morning this high air was quite cold, though the sun had begun to flush the sky eastward. A small crowd stood in the square, presenting their final messages to the passengers now entering the coach. There was a girl going down to marry an infantry officer, a whisky drummer from Kansas City, an Englishman all length and bony corners and bearing with him an enormous sporting rifle, a gambler, a solid-shouldered cattleman on his way to New Mexico and a slim blond man upon whom both Happy Stuart and the shotgun guard placed a narrow-eyed interest.

This seemed all until the blond man drew back from the coach door; and then a girl known commonly throughout the Territory as Henriette came quietly from the crowd. She was small and quiet, with a touch of paleness in her cheeks, and her dark eyes lifted at the blond man's unexpected courtesy, showing him a faint surprise. There was this small moment of delay and then the girl caught up her dress and stepped into the coach.

Men in the crowd were smiling but the blond one turned, his somber like the swift cut of a knife, and his sharp attention covered that group until the smiling quit. He was tall, lean-flanked, and definitely stamped by the guns slung low on his hips. But it wasn't the guns alone; something in his face, so watchful and so smooth, showed his trade.

Afterward he got into the coach and slammed the door.

Happy Stuart kicked off the brakes and yelled, "Hi!" Tonto's people were calling out their last farewells and the six horses broke into a trot and the stage lunged on its fore-and-aft springs and rolled from town with dust dripping off its wheels like water, the cavalrymen trotting briskly behind. So they tipped down the long grade, bound on a journey no stage had attempted during the last forty-five days. Out below in the desert's distance stood the relay stations they hoped to reach and pass. Between lay a country swept empty by the quick raids of Geronimo's men.

The Englishman, the gambler and the blond man sat jammed together in the forward seat, riding backward to the course of the stage. The drummer and the cattleman occupied the uncomfortable middle seat; the two women shared the rear seat. The cattleman faced Henriette, his knees almost touching her. He had one arm hooked over the door's window sill to steady himself. A huge gold nugget slid gently back and forth along the watch chain slung across his wide chest, and a chunk of black hair lay below his hat. His eyes considered Henriette, reading something in the girl that caused him to show her a deliberate smile. Henriette dropped her glance to the gloved tips of her fingers, cheeks unstirred.

THEY were all strangers packed closely together, with nothing in common save a destination. Yet the cattleman's smile and the boldness of his eyes were something as audible as speech, noted by everyone except the Englishman, who sat bolt upright in his corner, covered by a stony indifference. The army girl, tall and calmly pretty, threw a quick side glance at Henriette and afterward looked away with a touch of color. The gambler saw this interchange of glances and showed the cattleman an irritated attention. The whisky drummer's eyes narrowed a little and some inward cynicism made a faint change on his lips. He removed his hat to show a bald head already beginning to sweat; his cigar

smoke turned the coach cloudy and ashes kept dropping on his vest.

The blond man had observed Henriette's glance drop from the cattleman, and something bright disturbed his observant eyes; he tipped his hat well over his face and watched her—not boldly, but as though he were puzzled. Once her glance lifted and touched him. But he had been on guard against that, and was quick to look away.

The army girl coughed gently behind her hand, whereupon the gambler tapped the whisky drummer on the shoulder. "Get rid of that." The drummer appeared startled. He grumbled, "Beg pardon," and tossed the cigar through the window.

All this while the coach went tearing down the ceaseless turns of the mountain road, its heavy wheels slamming through the road ruts, whining at the turns, rocking interminably on its fore-and-aft springs. Occasionally the strident yell of Happy Stuart washed back: "Hi, Nellie! Hi, yit!" The whisky drummer braced himself against the door and closed his eyes.

Three hours from Tonto the road, making a last round sweep, let them down into the flat desert. Here the stage stopped and the men got out to stretch. The gambler spoke to the army girl gently: "Perhaps you would find my seat more comfortable." The army girl said, "Thank you," and changed over. The cavalry sergeant rode up to the stage, speaking to Happy Stuart.

"We'll be goin' back now—and good luck to ye."

The men piled in, the gambler taking the place beside Henriette. The blond man drew his long legs together to give the army girl more room, and watched Henriette's face. A hard sun beat fully on the coach and dust began to whip up like fire smoke. Without escort they rolled across a flat earth broken only by cacti standing against a dazzling light. In the far distance, behind a blue heat haze, lay the faint suggestion of mountains.

The cattleman reached up and tugged at the ends of his mustache and smiled again at Henriette. The army girl spoke to the blond man: "How far is it to the noon station?" he answered courteously: "Twenty miles." The gambler watched the army girl, something somber on his thin face, as though the run of her voice reminded him of things long forgotten.

THE miles fell behind and the smell of alkali dust got thicker. Henriette rested against the corner of the coach, her eyes dropped to the tips of her gloves. She made an enigmatic, disinterested shape there; she seemed past stirring, beyond laughter. She was young, yet she had a knowledge that placed the cattleman and the gambler and the drummer and the army girl in their exact places; and she knew why the gambler had offered the army girl his seat. The army girl was in one world and she was in another, as everyone in the coach understood. It had no effect on her, for this was a distinction she had learned long ago. Only the blond man broke through her indifference. His name was Malpais Bill, and she could see the wildness in the corners of his eyes and in the long crease of his lips; it was a stamp that would never come off. Yet something flowed out of him toward her that was different than the predatory curiosity of other men; something gallant, something gentle.

Up on the box Happy Stuart pointed to the hazy outline two miles away. "Injuns ain't burned that anyhow." The sun was directly overhead, turning the

Erny Haycox's story as it appeared in Collier's magazine

Ford, the famous director

a later interview, Ford would confess that he had paid only $2,500. In fact, the actual price was $1,500.

He first pitched the project to independent producer David O. Selznick. Selznick was dismissive. "It's a Western. People don't make Westerns anymore!" He was essentially right. In the 1920s Westerns had been churned out by the dozens because they made excellent action films. But when sound came to movies, producers and directors turned their attention to what they believed to be more sophisticated fare—and the old tradition of cowboy heroes in white hats and hissable villains in black hats was passé.

Ford was busy with other films: *The Hurricane*, featuring Jon Hall and Dorothy Lamour, and *Wee Willie Winkle*, starring Shirley Temple. But he found time to commission Dudley Nichols to come up with a screen treatment for "Stagecoach to Lordsburg." Dudley was less than enthusiastic. He thought the story was a mixture of *Grand Hotel*, *Covered Wagon*, and *The Iron Horse*. He began referring good-naturedly to the project as *The Grand Covered Iron Stagecoach*. Nichols finished the job in just a few weeks—and shortened the title to *Stagecoach*.

Ford took Nichols' treatment to Joe Kennedy at RKO, but met with no success. Ford then tried almost every other studio in town and the reaction was always the same: No one makes Westerns. Finally, he went to Walter Wanger, an independent producer who financed films with United Artists. Wanger was a longtime friend and Ford prevailed on that friendship to get Wanger to read the story. Wanger liked the idea and agreed to put up a quarter of a million dollars to finance the film, providing *Stagecoach* starred Gary Cooper and Marlene Dietrich.

With the reasonable certainty of funds available for production, Ford and Nichols went to work on a completed shooting script. Within a short time, they had hammered out a full screenplay. It took Haycox's "Stage to Lordsburg" to a new level of complexity and drama, and both men were confident that it had the makings of a great film.

THE MOVIE SCRIPT FOR *STAGECOACH*

After a scene establishing that Geronimo and his Apaches are on the warpath, a stagecoach in the town of Tonto in the Arizona Territory is boarded by seven people: Doc Boone, a whiskey-sodden old doctor; Hatfield, a former Confederate soldier who makes his living with cards; Dallas, a woman of ill repute with a checkered past; Mr. Gatewood, a banker who has stolen $50,000; Mr. Peacock, a quiet man who looks like a clergyman but who is actually a whiskey salesman; Lucy Mallory, the pregnant wife of an army officer; and Buck, an erratic stage driver. This diverse group of passengers is headed for Lordsburg, a route that takes them through Indian territory. Also on board is a marshal named Curly Wilcox who is searching for a fugitive called the Ringo Kid. Curly Wilcox knows that Ringo is on his way to Lordsburg to seek revenge on a man named Hank Plumber, who killed Ringo's father.

The stage comes across the Ringo Kid, whose horse has gone lame, and he is taken prisoner by the marshal as the stagecoach proceeds.

The stage arrives at Dry Fork, where they are informed that no cavalry is available to protect them on the journey ahead. Except for Mr. Peacock, they vote unanimously to risk the journey forward.

After the group arrives at Apache Wells, the pregnant Mrs. Mallory learns that her husband has been wounded and the shock sends her into labor. The alcoholic Doc Boone proves to be of little help and Dallas takes over the situation. After the group has sobered up Doc Boone, he finally assists in the delivery, but it is Dallas who becomes the heroine, as she emerges with the baby and stays with Mrs. Mallory through the night. Dallas and Ringo, the two misfits in the group, form

The stagecoach starts its journey.

an affectionate bond, and Ringo, on an evening walk, tells Dallas he would like to marry her. He tells her of his quest to kill his father's murderer and that if he succeeds he will probably go to jail. A confused Dallas runs away in tears. Ringo decides to escape, but when he sees signs of a pending Indian attack he returns to the camp.

The stagecoach continues on to Lee's Ferry, where passengers make the horrifying discovery that the station and the ferry have been burned and destroyed. The residents either have been killed or have fled. The group floats the coach with logs and navigates it across the river. They are soon attacked by a band of Apaches and Peacock is hit by an arrow. The group, which had been arguing before the attack, suddenly comes together to face the common danger. A full Indian attack gets under way.

The attack is ferocious and dramatic and things seem hopeless for the stagecoach and its passengers. They defend themselves with rifles and courage. When the horses run wildly, Ringo leaps from the stage and clambers over the rampaging animals until he can reach the lead horses. With the stage on the verge of being overwhelmed by the Indians, Hatfield decides to use his one remaining bullet to kill the praying Lucy Mallory in order to save her from the Apaches. The subsequent gunshot that is heard turns out to come from an Indian gun. It kills Hatfield and his gun falls from his hand. At that moment, a bugle sounds, heralding the arrival of the cavalry. The Apaches are routed as Ringo manages to bring the stagecoach under control.

The stage and its passengers finally arrive in Lordsburg. Mrs. Mallory and her baby are united with Lieutenant Mallory, who has survived his wound. Peacock is taken to the local doctor for treatment of his arrow wound. Greenwood, the bank thief, is taken under custody. Mrs. Mallory thanks Dallas in an awkward exchange, and marshal Curly Wilcox, in a gesture of gratitude for his heroism, gives Ringo his rifle and ten minutes to find Plumber and avenge himself. There ensues a teary and heartfelt departure scene between Ringo and Dallas.

At the local saloon, Hank Plumber and two of his brothers are playing poker when news arrives that Ringo is in town and looking for him. Plumber finds himself looking at a poker hand of aces and eights, recognized as the "dead man's hand." Plumber and his brothers exit the saloon to face Ringo. Shots are heard and Ringo's three bullets find their mark. Hank Plumber staggers back into the saloon and falls dead at the bar.

Ringo surrenders himself to the marshal, expecting to be put in jail, and he asks the lawman to take Dallas to the safety of his ranch. Ringo climbs aboard a wagon and says good-bye, but the marshal then invites Dallas to join Ringo and laughs as he permits Ringo to escape and to ride off with Dallas. As they ride away, Doc Boone philosophizes that they have been "saved from the blessings of civilization."

THE END

From "Stage to Lordsburg" to *Stagecoach*

Nichols' script had used the basic bones of the Haycox story and was faithful to Haycox's premise that the characters were "all strangers packed together with nothing in common save a destination." He kept the dangerous journey through Apache territory, the unlikely romance between a whore and a cowboy, and the avenging of a family murder. But the script altered the plot to give it more complexity and pathos, and it changed and dramatically enhanced the personalities aboard the stagecoach.

"Malpais Bill," the mysterious blond cowboy of Haycox's tale, became the avenging loner and escaped criminal, the Ringo Kid. The whiskey drummer and the gambler remained essentially the same but were given new names (Peacock and Hatfield) and more distinct personalities. Nichols added an alcoholic doctor (Doc Boone), a thieving banker (Gatewood), and a marshal (Curly Wilcox). And he impregnated

The stagecoach comes under attack as Ringo sounds the alarm.

the army wife (Mrs. Mallory). More important, he took the heroic cowboy off the original passenger list and put him further down the road where he would make his dramatic first appearance.

The movie script's addition of the childbirth scene not only adds drama to the story but permits the movie to portray and delineate the true character of the stage passengers. In Haycox's story, the Indian fight is a less important feature than in Nichol's script and does not take place until the stage is almost at its destination of Lordsburg. In the original story, several of the passengers are killed and there is no dramatic rescue by the cavalry. While there is no specific reference to time in the Haycox story, Nichols describes Hatfield as a recent Confederate soldier, thereby placing the story in the late 1860s.

Perhaps conscious of all the liberties that had been taken with Ernest Haycox's story, John Ford sent Haycox a bound copy of the shooting script on March 20, 1939. On the cover Ford wrote, "May I express my heartfelt thanks to the author of 'Stage to Lordsburg' in the hope that he was not disappointed with our attempt."

STAGECOACH HITS A SPEED BUMP

Just because Nichols and Ford were happy with the script did not mean they could automatically proceed. They still had a major hurdle to climb: the Hayes Office. Set up by the film industry earlier in the decade to monitor morality in motion pictures, the Hayes Office, under the direction of Joseph L. Breen, was the final arbiter of film scripts. Breen's calm demeanor belied his forceful character. Every major studio agreed to abide by his decisions. Sometimes, Breen killed movies in their infancy and they were never produced. More often, he objected to certain aspects of a script, which were then altered to obtain the stamp of approval.

Almost everything about the script of *Stagecoach* troubled Breen— the idea that a prostitute and a drunkard would both be portrayed sympathetically; that a man of the law would permit a criminal to shoot three people; that a convict would be shown to avoid the consequences of the law; that there was an abundance of whiskey drinking without

Dallas, Hatfield, Lucy Mallory, and Ringo ponder their fate.

consequences. He did not raise any objection to the portrayal of dozens of Native Americans being shot and killed.

In full panic mode, both Ford and Wanger hastened to assure the Hayes Office that the consumption of alcohol would be shown only as it was important to the plot; that the film would make clear that the character of Ringo would suffer pangs of conscience; that the words "prostitute," "harlot," or "whore" would never be used. Then Breen raised another concern: the political and economic philosophy running through the entire story. The banker, ordinarily seen as a contributor to society, was portrayed as an evil, hypocritical thief. The people who were ordinarily considered evildoers in films—the convict, the prostitute, and the drunkard—all turn out to be heroes. Ford pledged to play down the social content of the script as long as it did not damage the story. Just two weeks prior to the scheduled start of production, Breen acquiesced and gave *Stagecoach* the go-ahead.

Hayes Office Director Joseph L. Breen

CASTING THE STAGECOACH PASSENGERS

Production arrangements between Walter Wanger and other backers were settled in October of 1937, with Wanger putting up most of the money. The film was budgeted at $546,000, and in early November Wanger announced to the press, in true Hollywood fashion, that *Stagecoach* would be "a million dollar movie." The deal was more than fair to director John Ford—$50,000 plus a small percentage of the gross.

Ford set about casting the picture. He had long ago disabused Wanger of using Marlene Dietrich in the role of Dallas and had sold him on Claire Trevor. Trevor, at 29, was a veteran screen actress, specializing in "bad girl" roles and playing hard-bitten characters. Her more than

Claire Trevor

twenty film appearances had unhappily pigeonholed her as a star of "B" movies, but, in 1937, she had a breakout performance in *Dead End*, which earned her an Academy Award nomination as Best Supporting Actress. More important, in the pictures where Ford had directed her, she had impressed him as a sensitive and nuanced actress. Trevor happily signed on to *Stagecoach* for $15,000.

Casting for the role Ringo was another matter. Wanger had budgeted $3,000 for the male lead, and it was obvious that Gary Cooper was not going to work for that kind of money. Ford tested Bruce Cabot for the role, but Cabot was not impressive. Ford decided to consult one of his closest friends, Marion Morrison, to see if he had any ideas about who could do the role. Morrison and Ford had met on the set of a Ford film in 1926. Nicknamed "Duke" by his friends, Morrison was a tall, handsome, strong young man whom Ford liked and took under his wing. He began giving Morrison bit parts in films and eventually the young man was playing roles as a traditional film cowboy in a series of "quickie" "B" movies. He changed his name to John Wayne because he thought it was more memorable and looked better in the opening credits. Wayne had made sixty-five films in the 1930s, most of them produced on short budgets and timetables, all of them taking advantage of his strong male presence on the screen.

Ford, Wayne, Ward Bond, Dudley Nichols, and a few other friends formed a club they called "The Young Men's Purity Total Abstinence and Snooker Pool Association," and they frequently gathered on Ford's ketch, the *Araner*, for sails to Catalina Island. One morning in the early summer of 1938, as Ford and Wayne pulled out of the San Pedro harbor on a weekend cruise, Ford handed him Nichols' screenplay of *Stagecoach* and asked him to take a couple of hours and read it. That night at dinner, Ford said, "You know a

Marion Morrison

lot of young actors. Do you know anybody who could play the Ringo Kid?" Wayne replied, "Yeah. You should try to get Lloyd Nolan." The next day, Ford confronted Wayne again. "Too bad you never learned to act because you'd get better parts." Then he added, "Anyway, I want you to play Ringo." Wayne, who had resigned himself to a career of stereotypical roles in minor films, said later, "I felt as if I'd been hit in the belly with a baseball bat!"

The other roles for *Stagecoach* were filled from what had become almost a Ford stock company of actors: Donald Meek as Mr. Peacock, the timid whiskey drummer; John Carradine as Hatfield, the gambler; Thomas Mitchell as Doc Boone, the alcoholic doctor; George Bancroft as Curly Wilcox, the marshal; Berton Churchill as Mr. Gatewood, the thieving banker; Andy Divine as Buck, the stage driver. Wanger himself contributed the capable Louise Platt, whom he had under personal contract, for the role of Lucy Mallory, the pregnant wife of the unseen cavalry lieutenant. Ford scheduled production for forty-three days of filming, a condensed schedule by usual Ford standards, but one that was dictated by the strictures of Wanger's budget.

Finding the Great American West

In his new film, Ford was determined to portray the beauty and majesty of the land that had attracted the great Western migration and that had formed the character of the American cowboy. A search had uncovered a beautiful piece of land just west of Flagstaff, Arizona, for the filming of the outdoor scenes, and plans were under way for a production unit to begin filming there.

One afternoon a grizzled Indian trader showed up in the Ford office, asking to see the director. Told that he should leave because he didn't have an appointment, he said he would wait. Told that it would no doubt be a long wait, he announced that he was prepared for that and began untying his bedroll. Seeing that a problem was developing, the secretary wisely decided that an appointment did indeed exist and she showed the man into Ford's office. The man's name was Harry Goulding, and he had lived a large part of his life in a thirty-mile-wide strip of land along the Arizona and Utah border called Monument Valley. It was an area so remote that few Americans had ever seen it—located farther from a railroad station than any other place in America. It was here, said Goulding, that Ford should shoot his upcoming Western. Ford was dismissive until Goulding reached into his pouch and began showing him photographs. Ford quickly realized he was looking at his dream location—vast and spectacular, with sandstone mesas that rose into towers more than a thousand feet high. Virtually untouched by civilization, heroic in scale, never before recorded on film, it would make a perfect and frightening backdrop for the little stagecoach as it wended its way across hostile Indian territory. Monument Valley would help make *Stagecoach* a memorable movie—and *Stagecoach* would make Monument Valley famous.

Stagecoach Starts Its Journey

John Ford set his production schedule for two months of filming, and first on the agenda were the establishing shots at Monument Valley. On the last day of October 1938, Ford flew to Flagstaff and traveled overland to where he met his film crew and actors at the location. He learned to his delight that the local Navajo Indians were enthusiastic about a movie being made in their area and that they were willing laborers and happy to serve as extras. Ford, in fact, hired the tribe's medicine man to produce dramatic cloud formations during the filming.

Every morning, Ford would assemble all of the actors to go over the entire script for the day. This was a new experience for those who had not worked with Ford before. It was general studio practice for actors to be familiar only with their own scenes, but Ford wanted them to understand how their roles fitted into the overall scheme of the story. And he was always sharp with his criticism and demanding of top effort, even during the read-through.

Location shooting was wrapped up in just one week, consisting mostly of long establishing shots of the spectacular scenery and sequences of the stagecoach and the cavalry traveling the landscape, and of Indians in war paint and on horseback overlooking the stage from high bluffs. Then Ford spent two days filming the scene in which the Indians sweep down and pursue the coach as it speeds over the flats. One sequence, seen from the viewpoint of the coach, was shot from the top of a car. At one point, Ford thought the car was going unrealistically fast, but he was assured by the handlers that a team of six horses was perfectly capable of speeds over forty miles an hour.

Ford left the location with a sense of confidence. The shooting had gone well, and the scenery had been spectacular. Monument Valley had done its job.

The director hurried on with the other necessary location filming. The crew went to Kernville in northwestern California to film the river crossing scene and then moved on to Muroc Dry Lake near Victorville in southwest California. It was here that most of the Indian attack, the most dramatic sequence ever shot for a Western movie, was filmed. The action was fast and furious, as war-painted Indian extras mounted on fast-charging horses tried to bring down the fleeing stagecoach. The action involved Ringo getting the stage under control by leaping off the coach onto the backs of the rampaging horses and fighting his way over the teams until he reached the lead horses. Wayne was accustomed to doing much of his own stunt work in his previous films and was ready to do at least part of the scene. However, producer

Monument Valley, on the
Arizona/Utah border

Walter Wanger was present for the shooting at Muroc Dry Lake and, when he saw that Wayne was about to leap from the stagecoach, raised strong objections. Wanger had more than a quarter of a million of his own dollars invested in this film and he wasn't about to see the movie's star go down with an injury halfway through the shooting. Yakima Canutt, a former rodeo champion and now one of Hollywood's best stuntmen, was recruited to take over the honors. His heroics, caught on camera as he leaped from horse to horse while the stage raced over the lakebed, resulted in one of the most thrilling and exciting action scenes ever captured on early film.

Canutt also took the part of a marauding Indian who tries to stop the stage by leaping from his own horse onto the back of the lead horses. After being shot by Ringo, he was then required to fall between the horses. To everyone's relief, he managed to roll between the wheels of the stage as it passed over his body.

The Indian attack is true cinematic magic. It lasts a full seven-and-a-half minutes. Indians attack out of the hills, then fall with their horses by twos and threes as the stage passengers fire at them with pistols and rifles. At times, they seem to run right into the camera as they go down. Despite the fury and the dangers involved, there is no record of serious injury to either the horses or the riders involved.

California location shooting was wrapped up in four days and Ford and his crew packed up for their return to Hollywood. The rest of the film would be shot on studio sets—at MGM's special rear projection studio and at Republic's re-creation of a Western town.

Behavior on a Ford set was carefully circumscribed. Work started at nine o'clock sharp every morning. Ford would review the day's shooting with everyone involved, carefully rehearsing each scene before filming. Between shots an accordionist would play appropriate mood music to set a general tone and attitude on the set. Lunch was a communal affair with actors, cameramen, set people, and extras all eating together. Every afternoon there was a tea break. Except in emergency situations, filming ended every day at five o'clock.

This carefully organized routine did not mean Ford wasn't a tough taskmaster. He was all of that and more. He could be demanding, sarcastic, and insulting to his performers. Sometimes, he was downright abusive. His friend and *Stagecoach* screenwriter Dudley Nichols was almost always on the set, not just to suggest script changes but also to keep his boss under control and maintain calm. Some of the veteran actors knew how to handle Ford when he got too testy. At one point during the filming of Andy Devine driving the stagecoach, Ford yelled at him, "You big tub of lard, I don't know why I'm using you in this picture." Devine responded with "Because Ward Bond can't drive six horses." When he was too tough on Thomas Mitchell, Mitchell yelled back, "Just remember, I saw *Mary of Scotland*!"

But Ford was toughest on his friend and protégé John Wayne, trying to force a superb performance from him. He called him out as "a B actor," "a big oaf," and "a dumb bastard." He criticized the way Wayne walked in one scene, saying, "Walk like a man, for Christ's sake, instead of skipping like a fairy." And, "For Christ's sake, wash your face. You're just daubing it. Don't you ever wash at home?" It was tough on Wayne, but he took it, and he soldiered on and improved as he went. In his own way, Ford was transforming Wayne from a mediocre movie presence into a fine film actor.

Stuntman Yakima Canutt makes the leap.

Director Ford shooting a scene from *Stagecoach*

Filming on *Stagecoach* wrapped up two days before Christmas of 1938. Ford was just four days beyond his shooting schedule and had actually brought the film in under budget. It was a bravura performance for the director and his crew. Ford was pleased with the way things had gone—and so was producer Wanger.

GETTING STAGECOACH ON THE ROAD

It was known in the industry that Ford, unlike most directors, seldom interfered with the editing process. It was Ford's belief that a director could "edit in the filming." That is, the director made it so clear in the way he shot scenes that the footage would go together naturally and inevitably. However, with *Stagecoach*, he wanted to make sure everything came together the way he envisioned it, and he spent the better part of several days looking over editor Dorothy Spenser's shoulder.

He saw a number of things that bothered him. In several scenes, the shadow of a camera could be fleetingly seen, and in the stagecoach

Indians charge to attack the stagecoach.

chase, the shadow from a helicopter was briefly visible. Ford noticed that after the stagecoach plunged half-submerged through a muddy river, the passengers came out neatly pressed and unruffled. Ford wished he had messed them up a bit. In another scene, a van could be seen driving through a gate in the far distance. There was no way of re-shooting without incredible expense, so Ford hoped audiences would not notice or would quickly forget. All in all, he was pleased with what he saw.

Ford knew that *Stagecoach* required background music that would reflect the era and the genre, and a team of composers and arrangers, headed by Richard Hageman, put together a film score based on vintage songs like "Jeannie with the Light Brown Hair," "Bury Me Not on the Lone Prairie," and "Shall We Gather at the River." Ford commissioned a new theme to be written by an outside composer at a cost of $10,000, but the director was not happy with the result and it was scrapped. Producer Wanger kept his silence.

STAGECOACH TAKES THE STAGE

The final cut of *Stagecoach* ran ninety-six minutes, a length that Wanger knew would please theater owners. Top billing in the opening credits went to Claire Trevor, followed by John Wayne. The film was previewed on February 2, 1939, at the Fox Village Theater in Westwood. Because the theater was near UCLA, the audience was made up largely of college students. Wayne, visibly nervous, attended with a few friends and sat unobserved in the back of the theater in order to study audience reactions. Wayne's first appearance came fifteen minutes into the film and it was electric. Standing alone by the side of the road, holding his saddle and his Winchester rifle, Wayne filled the screen with authority and masculinity. It was, according to one historian, "one of the most stunning entrances in all of cinema." After that, the audience cheered almost every time he appeared. Said Wayne later, "They stomped, they screamed...nobody ever enjoyed a picture more than these people watching *Stagecoach*...it just had them mesmerized."

And then there was silence. After the preview, Wayne waited days before anyone at the studio commented. Wanger screened the film for some friends. Said one producer, "It's just a B picture." Another said, "It's all right, but it's still just a Western." Douglas Fairbanks Jr. simply said, "The chase is too long." Sam Goldwyn was even more dismissive, remarking, "Walter, you should have shot it in color. You ought to start all over and make it in color."

THE CRITICS CLIMB ON BOARD

Ford and Wanger were undeterred. On March 2, 1939, *Stagecoach* was released nationally, and the critics fell all over each other praising it. Frank Nugent of the *New York Times* was first out of the box: "In one superbly expansive gesture...John Ford has swept aside ten years of artifice and talkie compromise and has made a motion picture that sings a song of the camera. It moves, and how beautifully it moves ... nobly done...a stagecoach that's powered by a Ford." The *Hollywood Reporter* was equally effusive: "One of the greatest of all Westerns... superb entertainment...an example of consummate cinematic skill... continuously thrilling." The *National Board of Review Magazine* agreed: "*Stagecoach* is something for the true movie-lover to see more than once perhaps, for the story, again and again for delight in how the story is told."

Many of the reviewers, however, missed something important. They failed to see or to note something that audiences all across the country were witnessing: The birth of a great new movie star. John Wayne, often ignored in the glowing movie reviews for *Stagecoach*, had captured America's heart. When Wayne later walked into the offices of Republic studios, some of the secretaries began clapping—and soon all of them were standing and applauding. They knew something that the critics had missed. John Wayne had arrived.

STAGECOACH DELIVERS

The final total of all costs for producing *Stagecoach* added up to $531, 374, and its initial run returned more than $2 million—making it one of the hit movies of 1939. John Ford won the New York Critics Award as Best Director of the year and *Stagecoach* was nominated for seven Academy Awards, including Best Picture, Director, Supporting Actor, Cinematography, Musical Score, Editing, and Art Direction. However, like so many fine films that year, at the Oscar ceremony, *Stagecoach* was blown away by *Gone with the Wind*. Still, Thomas Mitchell won Best Supporting Actor for his alcoholic doctor and Richard

Trevor and Wayne on the set

Hagenian and his team won Best Musical Score.

In 1995, *Stagecoach* was deemed a "culturally, historically and aesthetically significant film" by the United States Library of Congress and was selected for preservation in its National Film Registry.

After Stagecoach

Ernest Haycox had a second film triumph in 1939 when his novel *Trouble Shooter* was the basis for Cecil B. DeMille's *Union Pacific*. Haycox continued his prolific output throughout the 1940s, with six more of his stories adapted to films, including *Sundown Jim* and *Canyon Passage*. Haycox died of cancer in 1951 at the age of fifty-one. He left behind an impressive legacy of twenty-five novels and more than three hundred short stories. In 2005, the Western Writers of America voted Haycox one of the best Western writers of the twentieth century.

* * *

In 1939, John Ford had one of the greatest years in motion picture history. In addition to *Stagecoach*, he directed *Young Mr. Lincoln*, *Drums Along the Mohawk*, his first color movie, and *The Grapes of Wrath*, for which he won the Academy Award. All four films have a firm place in movie history. In 1941, he won another Academy Award for *How Green Was My Valley*, one of the most highly nominated films of all time.

During World War II, Ford performed meritorious service in the United States Navy, filming a documentary, *The Battle of Midway*, during

John Wayne's iconic appearance as Ringo

which he was wounded by Japanese fire, and filming the fighting on D-Day during the attacks of the first wave of troops on Omaha Beach. For his actions he was cited for bravery under fire, and after the war he was named a rear admiral in the United States Naval Reserve.

Ford continued to make exceptional films during the 1950s and 1960s. His last great film was *The Man Who Shot Liberty Valance?* in 1962, starring John Wayne and Jimmy Stewart. When he finally retired in the late 1960s, John Ford had directed 140 motion pictures and won six Academy Awards, an achievement unequaled in movie history.

In 1972, he was honored by the Screen Directors Guild with its first Lifetime Achievement Award. That same year, he was made a full admiral by President Nixon, who also honored him with the Medal of Freedom. Ford died in 1973. Film critic Andrew Sarris wrote of Ford: "He was America's cinematic laureate."

✻ ✻ ✻

John Wayne, known to his friends as "Duke," went on from *Stagecoach* to become one of the greatest film stars of all time. His movie career lasted over half a century, and he made a number of iconic films in addition to *Stagecoach*: *Red River, Sands of Iwo Jima, The Quiet Man, The High and the Mighty, The Alamo, The Greatest Story Ever Told, True Grit,* and *Rooster Cogburn*. In all, Wayne appeared in nearly 250 films and had

a leading role in 142, a record that may never be broken. He was nominated for an Academy Award three times and won Best Actor for *True Grit*. He also won the Best Producer award for *The Apartment*.

By the time of his death from cancer in 1979, Wayne had become one of the most honored performers in film history. In his final year, the United States Congress awarded him the Congressional Medal of Honor and, in

John Wayne, movie star

Title card for *Stagecoach*

1990, a United States postage stamp was issued portraying John Wayne as the Ringo Kid in *Stagecoach*.

✶   ✶   ✶

Claire Trevor played opposite John Wayne twice immediately following their successful pairing in *Stagecoach*—in *Allegheny Uprising* and *Dark Command*. She continued her successful movie career over the next half century, appearing in more than seventy films. She won a second Academy Award in 1948 as Best Supporting Actress in *Key Largo*. In her later years, Trevor made a number of highly praised television appearances, winning an Emmy for her role in *Dodsworth* on Producers' Showcase. Trevor died in the year 2000 at the age of 90. Her name lives on in the Claire Trevor School of the Arts at the University of California, Irvine, where her Oscar and Emmy awards are on permanent display.

✶   ✶   ✶

Thomas Mitchell had the unusual honor of appearing as a featured actor in three of the greatest films in the greatest year in film history: as Doc Boone in *Stagecoach*, as Uncle Billy in *Mr. Smith Goes to Washington*, and as Gerald O'Hara in *Gone with the Wind*. Mitchell appeared in twenty-five films and was the first actor to win an Oscar, an Emmy, and a Tony Award. He died in 1962 at the age of seventy. Mitchell has two stars on the Hollywood Walk of Fame.

Orson Welles, preparing to direct his great film *Citizen Kane*, claimed to have watched *Stagecoach* every night for forty nights. Later, when asked in an interview who were his three favorite motion picture directors, Welles replied, "Ford, Ford and Ford."

Poster for *Stagecoach*

Stagecoach
The Final Facts

Studio:	United Artists
Executive Producer:	Walter Wanger
Director:	John Ford
Screenplay:	Dudley Nichols
Original Story:	Ernest Haycox
Cameraman:	Bert Glennon
Release Date:	March 2, 1939
Running Time:	96 minutes
Cost of Production:	$531,374
Box Office (original run):	$2,398,000

Cast

Ringo	John Wayne
Dallas	Claire Trevor
Doc Boone	Thomas Mitchell
Buck	Andy Devine
Hatfield	John Carradine
Mr. Peacock	Donald Meek
Curly Wilcox	George Bancroft
Lucy Mallory	Louise Platt
Lt. Blanchard	Tim Holt
Sgt. Billy Pickett	Francis Ford
Tom Tyler	Hank Plummer
Chris	Chris-Pin Martin
Mr. Gatewood	Berton Churchill
Cpt. Whitney	Cornelius Keefe
Ranchers	Buddy Roosevelt and Bill Cody
Indian Chief	Chief White Horse
Chief Big Tree	Yakima Canutt
Lucy's Baby	Mary Kathleen Walker

Awards

Academy Award Nominations: Best Picture, Best Director, Best Supporting Actor, Best Art Director, Best Musical Score, Best Cinematography (Black and White), Best Film Editing.

Academy Awards Won: Thomas Mitchell for Best Supporting Actor; Richard Hageman, Franke Harling, John Leipold, and Leo Shuken for Musical Score.

The manuscript of *The Gentleman from Montana*

MR. SMITH GOES TO WASHINGTON

THE STORY

Frank Capra leaned back in the chair in his office at Columbia Pictures and contemplated how it could have come to this. He would be leaving Columbia, his motion picture home for more than a decade. He had done great work, created some of the industry's most successful films, made money for himself and the studio, and achieved fame as a writer and director. And now, it was all coming to an end over an actress: Marlene Dietrich.

Capra had much to reflect on as he tried to make sense out of what had happened. He was not accustomed to failure—and hard work and good luck had always permitted him to overcome whatever obstacles had come his way.

He had more than triumphed over his humble start in life. Born in a small Sicilian village near Palermo, he had immigrated to America with his family in 1903. He would always remember his first sighting of the Statue of Liberty, and his father exclaiming, "Look at that!

Young Frank Capra

That's the greatest light since the star of Bethlehem. That's the light of freedom!" He had worked hard as the son of a Los Angeles fruit picker, been the first member of his family to ever go to college, served in the United States Army during World War I, and become a naturalized U.S. citizen after the war.

LYING HIS WAY INTO THE MOVIES

Dead broke and working at a menial job in San Francisco, Capra read a newspaper article about a new movie studio starting up in the city. He called the studio head and fabricated a story about being from Hollywood and having had experience as a film director. He told the lie well, and the man hired him to direct an inexpensive one-reel film for a fee of $75. Capra took to it like a fish to water and, using a group of amateur actors, knocked out the film in two days. His epic was called *The Ballad of Fultah Fisher's Boarding House*. It was shown in a small theater before a small audience and a few newspaper critics. To everyone's astonishment, especially Capra's, the film got rave notices the next day: "A very unusual single reeler...scenes all intensely dramatic...picture with dignity, beauty, and strength...strong acting... rapt audience attention...spontaneous applause." A flabbergasted Capra had found his life's work.

It wasn't long before Capra could say truthfully that he was from Hollywood. After stints in San Francisco as a prop man, a film editor, and a gag writer, Tinseltown finally beckoned in the form of Hal Roach, one of the town's leading producers of comedy films. Capra hit Hollywood running. Within just a few weeks, he had authored a number of "Our Gang" comedies. He soon transferred his talents to the Mack Sennett Studios, where he wrote and directed a number of successful short films and, almost single-handedly, made a great comedic star out of Harry Langdon. Then came the call he had been waiting for: Harry Cohn of Columbia Pictures wanted to talk to him.

Hollywood producers in the late 1920s were desperate for talent, and Harry Cohn was as desperate as any of them. Cohn was an almost cartoonish Hollywood character. Arrogant, brash, loudmouthed, and self-centered, he ran his Columbia studio like a personal fiefdom. He also ran it on a shoestring. While the larger studios of MGM and Warner Brothers were spending hundreds of thousands of dollars on films, using their own established banks of stars, Cohn and Columbia were turning out short subjects, travelogues, cartoons, and sports reels with budgets as low as $1,500 a film. Cohn knew how to make money, but now he lusted after respectability. He wondered if Capra could be his ticket to the big time.

Young Harry Cohn

Capra was as ambitious as Cohn and he was in just as much of a hurry. He was thirty years old and he felt as if life was passing him by.

Capra's introduction to Cohn was classic Hollywood. When he first walked into Cohn's office at Columbia, Capra found Cohn having sex with one of his aspiring actresses. Cohn casually waved Capra away and asked him to come back in a few minutes. (Cohn's casting couch would later reach legendary status. After he signed a long-term contract with Rita Hayworth, he suggested they seal the deal with a little sex. Hayworth carried the day, saying "Keep your pants on, Harry. I'm having lunch tomorrow with your wife and daughters!")

THE PARTNERSHIP

After some initial jousting, Capra and Cohn eventually found accommodation. Each wanted what the other had. Capra needed someone who had the power to let him write and direct the films he wanted to make. Cohn wanted someone with the talent and ability to turn out films that would both make money and please the critics. Capra wanted fame and acclaim; Cohn wanted money and respect. Over the next ten years, they would hugely reward each other while, at the same time, make movie history.

**The legendary movie team
of Cohn and Capra**

Their relationship was not always a pleasant one. Capra referred to Cohn as "the monster" and said, "Just his presence would make your hackles rise and your adrenals pump furiously. He annoyed and belittled until he made you hate him." For his part, Cohn always called Capra "dago" and seemingly did everything he could to make Capra's life miserable. If Capra said he needed $50,000 to make a picture, Cohn would cut it in half. If Capra wanted two months to shoot a film, Cohn would cut the schedule to six weeks. If Capra requested fifteen extras for a scene, Cohn would send seven. Still, they managed to work together and make money for Columbia. From 1927 to 1937, they combined their talents to produce more-than-adequate, nicely profitable movies with such forgettable titles as *That Certain Way*, *So This Is Love*, *Flight*, and *The Matinee Idol*.

But then something strange, wonderful, and frightening happened to motion pictures. In a movie called *The Jazz Singer*, Al Jolson had opened his mouth and the sounds of his hit song "Mammy" had wafted out over the audience. It was a miracle. Suddenly, pictures not only moved, they also talked and sang. Confusion reigned over Hollywood. Some thought sound in movies was just a fad. Others believed it would be useful only in musical numbers. Capra knew better. He sensed immediately that it was a revolution and that he might be uniquely qualified to take advantage of it. As a young man, he had worked his way through college at the California Institute of Technology. He had worked as a technician in every phase of moviemaking. He was sure he knew how to use sound to make better pictures.

Capra's first "talkie" was a compromise between what he wanted to do and how much money Cohn would give him to do it. The first half of *The Younger Generation* was shot as a silent film at the Columbia studios, the second half was shot in sound in the town of Santa Monica. The hybrid film turned a profit, and Capra and Cohn never looked back.

HUMILIATION AT THE ACADEMY AWARDS

In 1933, Capra put together and directed a film called *Lady for a Day*. It was based on a Damon Runyan story about a New York fruit seller called "Apple Annie," whose daughter was raised and educated abroad and was in the mistaken belief that she was the offspring of a wealthy society matron. The film had heavy social content, surprising twists and turns, and a tear-inspiring finale. Audiences loved it, critics adored it, and it was nominated for four Academy Awards, including Best Director. Capra was certain he had finally gained respectability and the affection of his Hollywood peers. He ordered his first tuxedo and wrote out a moving and grateful acceptance speech. He would be ready.

The Academy Award ceremony that year was held at the Biltmore Hotel. The master of ceremonies was a friend of Capra's, Will Rogers. As the evening wore on, Capra sat and waited impatiently until the directing award came due. Rogers began "... and the award for best director of the year is ... the envelope please ... yes, here it is. Well, well, well, what do you know! I've watched this young man for a long time ... saw him come up from the bottom, and I mean the bottom. It couldn't happen to a nicer guy. Come up and get it, Frank!"

Frank Capra at the Oscars

Capra leaped to his feet as his table broke into cheering and applause. Capra was halfway up the aisle when Rogers finally exclaimed, "Frank Lloyd!" As the spotlight hit Lloyd, Capra stumbled back to his table in the dark as someone yelled, "Down in front!" That night Frank Capra got very drunk.

CAPRA HITS THE JACKPOT

Capra bandaged up his wounds and soldiered on. He had another movie to make. Hollywood was having a laugh at his expense, but now he was more determined than ever to win its applause.

Next up for Capra was a movie called *Night Bus*. The script was based on a magazine story by Samuel Hopkins Adams that Capra had purchased for $5,000. The plot involved a romance that takes place during a long bus ride. Capra had trouble casting the lead performers. Myrna Loy, Margaret Sullivan, Miriam Hopkins, and Constance Bennett all turned it down. Finally, after promising to make the movie in just six weeks, he persuaded Claudette Colbert to take the lead female role. However, casting the male lead also presented some problems.

Capra decided he wanted MGM to lend him its star performer, Robert Montgomery, for the role. MGM refused but came back offering another of its lesser-known actors. Capra had seen him in only one movie, in which the actor had played a "tough guy" role. Capra had not been impressed. Cohn told him to stop whining and take the offer, and so Capra reluctantly said yes to Clark Gable. A few days later, Capra was even less impressed when Gable reported to Columbia dead drunk.

Capra wound up shooting the movie in just four weeks at a Cohn-induced budget of just $350,000. When Cohn reviewed the finished product, he was not happy. The movie, after Capra had edited it, was two hours long—too long, Cohn believed, to make theater owners happy. Capra stuck by his guns and Cohn finally gave in. Cohn hated the title, *Night Bus*, claiming that two other recent films about bus trips had flopped at the box office. He wanted the word "bus" out of the title. This time, Cohn won the argument. Capra renamed the movie *It Happened One Night*.

At the Academy Awards ceremony the following year, *It Happened One Night* won all the major awards: Best Picture, Best Actress, Best Actor, and Best Director. It was an unprecedented grand sweep. As Claudette Colbert held her trophy in her arms, she said in a firm voice, "I owe Frank Capra for this!" When his turn came, Capra walked proudly and slowly to the stage—this time in the spotlight.

Poster of *It Happened One Night*

Later that night, after the celebrating was over, he did exactly what he had done the year before. He got drunk. But this time he did it clutching his Oscar.

BETRAYAL

The next five years were halcyon days at Columbia. Cohn and his studio continued to turn out profitable potboilers, including the immensely popular "Three Stooges" films. And Capra continued producing quality moneymaking movies. Because of his popularity with theatergoers, Capra was able to write a contract with Cohn that entitled him to put his name above the title of his films. Thus, his next films were billed as "Frank Capra's *You Can't Take It with You*," "Frank Capra's *Lost Horizons*," and "Frank Capra's *Mr. Deeds Goes to Town*." His name itself had become an advertisement for his films.

In 1938, Capra decided to reward himself with an extensive European vacation. During his stop in London, a friend called his hotel to congratulate him on the successful run of his new hit film, *If She Could Only Cook*. Capra was flattered by the compliment, except for one thing—he had never heard of *If She Could Only Cook*.

When he went to Columbia's London office to find out what was going on, he was congratulated again by the manager who handed him a playbill for the movie. There it was in black and white: "Frank Capra's *If She Could Only Cook*." He went to a theater for further confirmation and there it was again on the screen! How could it be possible that his name was on a film he had nothing to do with? There was only one possible answer: Harry Cohn.

As soon as Capra returned to Hollywood, he stormed into Cohn's office and demanded to know what the hell Cohn thought he was doing. Cohn was only moderately defensive, telling Capra he just wanted to make more money on the movie's overseas run. Wasn't that why they were both making movies? Maybe they should put Capra's name on more films if it would make them more profitable. Cohn would be happy to cut Capra in on any additional income produced by the use of his name on other future films. Capra was apoplectic. He stormed out of the office, after telling the studio boss that it would be impossible for them to work together anymore. He was leaving Columbia. Cohn yelled back that Capra was still under contract and that he wasn't about to release him to work for any other studio.

The result was an impasse—and a flurry of lawsuits. After more than two years of claims and counterclaims, the lawyers were still arguing and the courts were still pondering. Capra had not made a film in three years, and Columbia was starting to hurt. Finally, Cohn gave in and asked his prize director to return to the fold. He had a film for him to direct. It was called *Chopin*. Capra heaved a sigh of relief and took up the task.

THE FIGHT OVER MARLENE DIETRICH

The relationship between Capra and Cohn was now extremely brittle. It wouldn't take much to shatter it again. Capra had long wanted to do a biopic of the great composer and he eagerly set about working on the script with his writers. In the meantime, Cohn planted a story in Luella Parsons' column that he was soliciting advice from the public on who should play the lead roles, even suggesting the name of Rosalind Russell for

Marlene Dietrich

the role of George Sand. This was the kind of thing that drove Capra to distraction. He regarded casting in his films as an important prerogative. He had his own idea of who should play Frédéric Chopin and George Sand: Charles Boyer and Marlene Dietrich. He confronted Cohn on the subject.

"No way," replied Cohn. "Dietrich is box office poison." Capra pressed his point: "It's lousy pictures that are poison at the box office, not actors. Anyway, Dietrich plays George Sand or I'm out!" Cohn wouldn't relent. "Okay, you're out." Capra raged out of Cohn's office, hurried back to his own office, and slammed the door. It was over. He would leave Columbia for good.

THE GENTLEMAN FROM MONTANA

As he sat back in his chair, reflecting on the past, he also thought about the future. Finally, he asked his secretary to send "his gang" up to the office. He was leaving Columbia and he hoped they would go with him. After Capra had announced the news, Joe Sistrom, Capra's top assistant, said, "Wait a minute! Read this." He handed Capra two pages of lined yellow paper, saying, "I just read a book called *The Gentlemen from Montana* by Lou Foster." Capra recognized the name immediately. Foster was one of Hollywood's top story creators and scriptwriters. Capra read the two pages hurriedly and jumped to his feet. It was the kind of patriotic, idealistic, sentimental story he loved. He concluded almost immediately that it was a film he had to make—even if it meant one more movie with Cohn and Columbia. "Can you buy it?" Capra asked. "For a lunch at the Brown Derby," was Sistrom's answer.

Sistrom knew that Foster needed a boost to his career. Working under his full name of Lewis R. Foster, he had had considerable early success in Hollywood as a gag writer and film director at both the Hal Roach and Mack Sennett studios. Some of his films, such as *The Merry Widower*, *Stolen Harmony*, and *Two in a Crowd*, had been profitable and well reviewed. But film writing was a chancy business, and now Foster was freelancing and doing his best to support his wife and two children. He decided to try something new—writing a completely original story. He came up with a serviceable plot: A naive and idealistic Boy Scout leader suddenly becomes a United States senator when he is appointed

Lewis R. Foster

on a whim by his state's governor. Once in Washington, the new senator becomes enthralled and overwhelmed by the city's beauty and history. Then he comes up against his state's senior senator and discovers the political process is not what he thought it should be. In his attempt to establish a national boy's camp, he runs headlong into corruption and backbiting. With the help of his female assistant, he triumphs over the system, as a result of a dramatic and patriotic speech on the U.S. Senate floor.

Foster was a quick study and accustomed to working with

deadlines, and he turned out his story in just a couple of weeks. He immediately set about in search of a book publisher while he worked the movie studios. Both Paramount and MGM passed on his story, so he took it to Reuben Mamulian, a director at Columbia. Mamulian was a recently naturalized American and had a great affection for his new country and its traditions. He loved the storyline of *The Gentleman from Montana* and took it to Harry Cohn with a recommendation that Columbia buy the story. Cohn was dismissive: "That's already been looked at—at other studios. It can't be any good." Mamulian was equally resolute: "If you don't want it, I'll buy it and make my own movie!" It was a hollow gesture. Instead, Mamulian circulated the story around Columbia.

When it landed on his desk, Joe Sistrom spotted immediately that it was Capra's kind of story. He wrote a two-page synopsis and waited for a chance to enthuse his boss. He was right. Capra was already pacing the room, spouting ideas to his staff, and he asked Sistrom, "You sure you can get this that cheap? Do whatever it takes."

As it turned out, Sistrom was wrong about the price being a lunch at the Brown Derby. But not by much. It cost Columbia a check for $1,500. Foster gave up the movie rights so easily because he knew what it would mean to have his name on a successful Capra film. It would simply ignite his career.

Capra's crew originally believed the movie could be a successful sequel to *Mr. Deeds Goes to Town*, an earlier Capra film about a character similar to the one in Foster's story. That film had starred Gary Cooper in the lead role. If Cooper was available, this new movie could be called *Mr. Deeds Goes to Washington* and could hitchhike on the popularity of the earlier film. But Cooper was not available. He was under contract and committed to two more films. Capra was almost relieved, because all along he had really had his heart set on Jimmy Stewart, whom he felt had the kind of freshness and innocence on the screen that would play perfectly against the craftiness and political heavy-handedness that the character would be up against in Washington. And Capra had just finished a successful film, *You Can't Take It with You*, with Stewart and he enjoyed working with the young actor.

Young Jimmy Stewart

STEWART COMES ON BOARD

Jimmy Stewart had started his acting career on the New York stage, where his lanky physique, good looks, boyish charm, and soft Midwestern voice soon won over audiences. MGM signed him to a contract in 1934, and he quickly appeared in several films in uncredited bit parts. The studio had difficulty casting him because of his unusual slow and hesitant way of speaking, a style which would later become his world-famous trademark. Finally, he got his chance in a major role in *The Murder Man,* and his popularity with moviegoers in that film encouraged MGM to give him star turns in additional films, like *Born to Dance* and *After the Thin Man.* Capra took notice of him at that point and signed Stewart on for a top role in *You Can't Take It with You.* Stewart played the lead role of Tom Kirby, a sentimental and honest man, whose character holds the plot together. He was superb in the role, received great reviews, and won the admiration of director Capra. Stewart was currently unassigned at MGM and the studio was willing to lend him to Columbia. Stewart eagerly signed on for Capra's new film.

Jean Arthur was Capra's almost automatic choice to play the beautiful, wisecracking, know-it-all assistant to the fledgling senator. Arthur was a Capra "discovery." One day while passing the projection room, he heard a

Jean Arthur

woman's voice that he later remembered as "low, husky, that sometimes broke into a higher register like a thousand tinkling bells." He stuck his head into the room and on the screen he saw a "lovely young woman, simple, real, vibrant." He decided on the spot he wanted her for the female lead opposite Gary Cooper in *Mr. Deeds Goes to Town*. He signed her for the role over Harry Cohn's objections, and she turned out to be a ten strike. Arthur became an overnight star, and now Capra wanted her for his new picture. Like Stewart, she signed on eagerly. With Cooper not in the picture, the idea of making a sequel to the "Deeds" film was rejected and the project was renamed *Mr. Smith Goes to Washington*.

MR. CAPRA GOES TO WASHINGTON

Capra flew off to the nation's capital with veteran writer Sidney Buchman to scout for scenes for the film. Capra was almost as enthralled and bedazzled on his first trip there as the character in his film would be. On a sightseeing bus, Capra saw Washington just as a dewy-eyed freshman senator would see it: the Capitol, the Supreme Court, the White House, Arlington Cemetery, the Lincoln Memorial, and the Washington Monument. His enthusiasm grew with each stop. Finally, Capra visited the Senate Chamber where so much of the film's action would take place. It was the perfect setting he had envisioned, a venue filled with history and beauty. But there was a problem: Photography of any kind was forbidden in its hallowed halls. Capra would have to build his own Senate in Hollywood. It would have to be a perfect replica down to every detail—the senators' chairs, the vice-presidential chair, the paintings, the press gallery, the uniforms of the attendants, even the names carved into the tables where the senators sat. It would be a heroic task, and he would have to talk Harry Cohn out of more money than he had budgeted for the film. He would eventually argue Cohn out of $2 million, making "Mr. Smith" Columbia's most expensive picture ever.

Returning to Hollywood, Capra ran headlong into an unforeseen problem. Someone at Columbia had discovered that author Maxwell Anderson had earlier written a book called *Both Your Houses,* with a plot somewhat similar to that of *The Gentleman from Montana*.

Capra's Senate Chamber

Columbia's lawyers were fretting that it had the makings of a lawsuit, especially if the movie turned out to be a big moneymaker. With his film at risk, Capra talked Cohn into buying the film rights to *Both Your Houses* as protection against future litigation. The studio paid Maxwell Anderson $23,000, more than ten times what they had paid for the story they were actually going to use.

Construction of the set got under way in the summer of 1939. The art director, Lionel Bowles, working with ancient Capitol blueprints and hundreds of photographs, spent one hundred days and employed the talents of several architects and hundreds of carpenters in duplicating the iconic Senate Chamber. When he finished, he had produced an exact duplicate of the chamber, down to the clock on the wall and the scratches on the desks. In the niched walls behind the Senate Gallery were the carved busts of twenty vice presidents. Then Bowles set about duplicating the Senate cloakrooms, committee rooms, antechambers, and offices. The finished set was so exact and so impressive that, when

Capra walked into it, he felt the same sense of awe that he felt when he first found himself in the real thing.

One of the reasons the set was so accurate in every detail was that Capra had hired James Preston, the official press officer of the United States Senate Gallery, to be on hand during construction and to be present at the filming of the scenes in the Senate. Preston turned out to be a goldmine of information and a stickler for accuracy.

THE STORY BECOMES A SCRIPT

The writing of the film script was wrapping up, and a number of changes had been made from Foster's original story. In order not to offend or praise any particular state, Mr. Smith became the new senator from a state with no name. Jefferson Smith, the hero of the story, was a Boy Scout leader in the story, but Capra couldn't obtain permission from the National Scout Headquarters to use its name in the film. So Smith became a "Boy Ranger" leader.

Buchanan and Capra generally followed Foster's plot, but they flushed it out with a number of dramatic sequences, including Jefferson Smith's cab ride through Washington, during which he marvels at all the great buildings and monuments. They also enhanced and romanticized the relationship between Smith, the new senator, and his assistant, Clarissa Saunders, so that she goes from pitying him to loving him.

While Capra was on his trip to Washington, D.C., he had visited the Lincoln Memorial and heard a young boy read the inscriptions on the monument to his elderly grandfather, who had vision problems. The event was written into the script as witnessed by Smith during his first trip there. The result was one of the most moving scenes in the film.

THE MOVIE SCRIPT FOR
MR. SMITH GOES TO WASHINGTON

A United States senator from an unidentified Western state dies unexpectedly from a heart attack. The state's governor, Hubert ("Happy") Hopper, must appoint a new senator to replace him. A corrupt political boss, James Taylor, sees it as an opportunity to have an easily manipulated patsy named in his place, thereby furthering his scheme to have a land-grabbing bill passed through the Senate. However, there is a public demand to name a responsible, honest man to the position. At a dinner in his home, the governor is harassed by his children to appoint Jefferson Smith, their Boy Ranger leader and the owner of a local pet store. The governor finally decides to flip a coin to decide between Jefferson and another candidate. The coin lands on its edge—directly next to a newspaper article about Jeff Smith. The governor decides it is an omen and makes the appointment of Smith.

The state's senior senator, Joseph Paine, discovers that Smith is the son of an old, departed friend, and so he takes Smith under his wing. Unfortunately, Paine has long been under the control of Taylor, the scheming political boss. The older senator and Smith travel to the nation's capital on a train together. During the ride, Smith learns that his father long ago fought Taylor and his corrupt politics, failed, and died a martyr to the cause of honesty and justice.

After he arrives in Washington, Smith takes a long bus tour of its sites and monuments. He is impressed and awed as he views the Lincoln Memorial, the Washington Monument, the Tomb of the Unknown Soldier, and the archived Declaration of Independence. At the Lincoln Monument, he hears a young lad reading Lincoln's words aloud.

At the Capitol building, Mr. Smith meets Clarissa Saunders, a member of the senior senator's staff, who has been tasked with showing Smith the ropes and keeping him busy with trivial matters. In the meantime, the city's newspapers have begun ridiculing Smith as a country bumpkin, out of his league in the Capitol. Smith's worshipful tour of the city becomes fodder for their ridicule, and Smith seeks revenge by seeking out his persecutors, which only makes his situation worse. Among his tormenters is a hard-drinking reporter, Diz Moore, who is in love with Saunders.

Smith decides to learn the ropes of his Senate position and begins a determined study of how laws are shaped and how he should vote on them. To keep Smith occupied on lesser matters, Paine, the senior senator, suggests he come up with his own bill, something insignificant

Stewart as the new senator

and unpromising like a bill proposing a boys' camp in his home state. Smith astounds Paine by coming up with the bill overnight, with the aid of Saunders, who has become infatuated with Smith's honesty and character. Paine is then horrified to find that the site Smith has chosen for the camp is the same one where he and the political boss, Taylor, have planned to build a dam that would greatly enrich their landholdings.

To keep Smith away from the Senate when the dam bill comes up for a vote, Paine enlists the services of his attractive daughter to entice Smith on a romantic adventure. This scheme is averted by Saunders, who shows Smith some correspondence that exposes the scheme.

Smith confronts Paine on the subterfuge and is astonished to find that the man he has so greatly admired is truly corrupt and is in Taylor's pocket. When bribery and threats do not work on Smith, Paine and Taylor decide to frame him. On the Senate floor, Paine accuses Smith of owning the land on which the boys' camp will be established, and he displays falsified documents to support his charges. Smith tries to deny the charge but is booed off the floor by his fellow senators. At a later hearing, the falsified documents are used to further intimidate him. Smith walks out of the hearing, totally disillusioned, determined to depart Washington for good.

Before leaving Washington, Smith revisits the Lincoln Memorial and sits on its steps, filled with sad thoughts and seemingly devoid of his lofty ideals. Saunders finds him there and encourages him to return to the Senate and fight the good fight.

Smith arrives at the chambers just as roll call is being taken and the motion to expel him from the Senate comes up for a vote. Smith demands to be heard, and once he has the floor, he refuses to yield, despite demands from the other senators. Suddenly, it dawns on him that as long as he continues speaking he cannot be forced to yield. With help from Saunders, who encourages him from the Senate Gallery with coaching and hand signals, he defends himself forcefully and eloquently. When other senators, led by Paine, walk out on him, Smith is undeterred. Fortified by coffee and sandwiches from his desk, he launches a seemingly unstoppable filibuster. James Taylor, the machine politician, rails at Smith from his own desk, but Smith counters with telling logic and high emotion, quoting from the Bible, the Constitution, and the Bill of Rights. His eloquence and fighting spirit carry the day with the returning senators, as Smith keeps up his verbal barrage for a full twenty-four hours. Weak of voice and exhausted, he finally collapses on the Senate floor.

Arthur, Stewart, and Mitchell in a still photo from the filming

Paine is so moved and so consumed with guilt that he rushes out of the Senate and attempts to commit suicide. Failing that, he rushes back to the Senate floor and purges his soul, admitting that everything Smith has said about him and Taylor is the truth and that they had attempted to frame Smith in order to prevent him from revealing their own schemes.

Clarissa Saunders rushes to the collapsed Smith and breathes a sigh of relief when she sees that he has survived his ordeals. She confesses her love for him as the Senate becomes a place of cheering bedlam. The vice president attempts to restore order with his gavel, but finally gives up and leans back in his chair with a look of satisfaction on his face.

Jefferson Smith and Clarissa Saunders, now portrayed as a couple, return from Washington to Smith's hometown, planning a future together. They are met by a band and cheering locals and are then engulfed in a ticker tape parade down the city's main street,

Jefferson Smith confronts Senator Paine.

saluting the now-celebrated accomplishments of the state's new senator. Later, Smith climbs on his motorcycle and goes to Senator Paine's house where they reunite and discuss how Taylor's political machine has been exposed and crushed, thanks to their combined efforts and by actions of the Senate. Smith and Saunders then go to Smith's mother's home on the motorcycle, where Saunders is emotionally embraced and welcomed as a member of the family.

THE END

HOW THE SCRIPT ALMOST DIED

In 1938, Foster's novel, *The Gentleman from Montana*, had been submitted to the censors of the Hayes Office for advance approval of the story line. This was a precautionary step sometimes taken by studios if they foresaw any future controversy regarding a

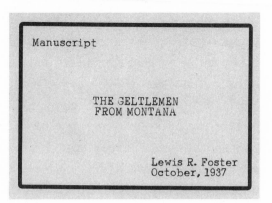

Manuscript

THE GELTLEMEN
FROM MONTANA

Lewis R. Foster
October, 1937

Label of *The Gentleman from Montana*

plotline. Word had come back from the censorial body that troubled the studio: "We most earnestly urge that you take serious counsel before embarking on the production of any motion picture based on this story. It looks to us like one that might well be loaded with dynamite both for the motion picture industry and for the country at large. The generally unflattering portrayal of our system of government might well lead to such a picture being considered both here and, more particularly, abroad as a covert attack on the democratic form of government."

The Hayes Office had the power to kill a picture with a simple adverse ruling, but Columbia and Capra went ahead with their plans despite the danger. However, they were still cautious. After the script was completed, they submitted it for approval—and the Hayes Office changed its position, stating, "It is a grand yarn that will do a great deal of good for all those who see it. It is particularly fortunate that this kind of story is to be made at this time. Out of Senator Jeff's difficulties there has been evolved the importance of a democracy." This complete reversal of attitude allowed Capra and Columbia to breathe a collective sigh of relief.

FILLING OUT THE ROLES

With Stewart and Arthur set for the starring roles in "Mr. Smith," casting for the lesser roles went relatively smoothly. It was, nevertheless, a big job. The script called for 186 speaking parts. To play the role of the senior senator from Smith's unnamed state, the story's villain-hero, Capra signed up veteran actor Claude Rains. The part of the political boss went to Edward Arnold, an actor experienced in portraying hard-hearted characters. The role of the governor who appoints Smith to the Senate went to pop-eyed, phlegmatic Guy Kibbee. Assigning the part of Diz, the heavy-drinking newspaper man who lusts after Saunders, took some time. Capra got it into his head that he wanted a left-handed actor. His feeling was that a southpaw appeared inherently offbeat and unpredictable in scenes, opening doors the wrong way, drinking with the wrong hand. After a search of lefties, the job went to Thomas Mitchell, who was already signed up for a later role as Scarlett O'Hara's father in *Gone with the Wind*.

Given his obsession with authenticity, Capra had U.S. Senate expert Jim Preston help in the casting of all ninety-eight extras who would fill the Senate seats in the final scene of the film. The roles of the governor's eight rambunctious children who bully him into appointing Smith to the Senate went to eight actual siblings from an acting family named Watson.

With the script now in hand, with the blessing of the Production Code, and with the cast selected and signed, Capra pushed ahead on production, using a $2 million budget coaxed out of Harry Cohn. It would be the most expensive film in Columbia history—and the stakes were big. On April 3, 1939, filming got under way.

CHALLENGES ON THE SET

The newly created Senate Chamber was a boxed-in, four-sided set, surrounded by a continuous rectangle of gallery and press seats. The confined space had been built without a real contemplation of the problems it would present for lighting and for camera movements. When Capra started setting up his shooting schedule, he realized he had a nightmare on his hands. He would have to record and film hundreds of scenes almost simultaneously on three levels while moving tons of heavy equipment with each setup. Working with his cameraman, Joe Walker, his head electrician, George Hager, and his sound engineer, Ed Bernds, Capra devised a multiple-camera, multiple-sound channel

A thoughtful Frank Capra on the set

method of shooting that could film up to six separate scenes with a single equipment move. It was an innovation that years later Capra would regret not patenting.

Because there were so many close-ups of the actors that had to be created, and because realism was so important, Capra came up with another innovation. Actors were accustomed to speaking their close-ups with just the director and technicians present. They would recite their lines out of sequence and without anyone to react to. Frequently, directors would have a stagehand or a script girl read the line the actor was supposed to be responding to. Capra was not getting the performances from his actors that he wanted using this system, so he began using the recorded voice of the other actor or actors into which the new voice was to be fitted. That way, the actor doing his close-up lines felt as if he was actually a part of the previously shot scene. It worked perfectly and Capra got the performances he wanted.

THE PROBLEM OF JEAN ARTHUR

Then there was the problem of Jean Arthur's face. No one, of course, has an absolutely asymmetrical face. Actors and actresses frequently favor one side or the other and try to show their best side in their stage or film appearances. But Arthur was a special case. As Harry Cohn once said, somewhat cruelly, "D'ja ever look at her face? Half of it's angel. The other half is a horse."

Jean Arthur shows
her best side

Capra had already had a similar problem years earlier in filming Claudette Colbert in *It Happened One Night*. Colbert insisted that the left side of her face be shown in every scene, causing innumerable difficulties in staging and filming setups. As one cameraman said, "The right side of Colbert's face is like the dark side of the moon. You know it's there even though you've never seen it."

To keep Arthur's problem to a minimum, Capra actually had some of the smaller sets of rooms and hallways constructed to permit her to enter from the right. His theory was that if she were initially positioned to face forward or look to her left, she would make instinctive and awkward moves to show her favored side. Capra wanted his female star to be confident and relaxed as she moved about the set. A study of the finished movie shows that in "Mr. Smith," the audience is looking at the left side of Arthur's face about 90 percent of the time. In several of her scenes, she is in full profile.

Capra also had to deal with Arthur's emotional problems. She was, Capra said, plagued with the worst case of stage fright he ever saw. Before every shot, Arthur would have to be coaxed out of her dressing room, and even then she would find a hundred reasons why she wasn't quite ready. She would visibly tremble and sometimes have to be pushed into the scene. However, when the camera rolled, "she would transform from a whiney mop into a warm, lovely, poised, and confident actress—like a cockroach," said Capra, "turned into a butterfly." Then, when the scene was over, she would rush to her dressing room and lock the door. Frequently, the sound of vomiting could be heard.

Capra was willing to pay the price of Arthur's histrionics because her contributions to the success of the film were so great. There is a long, one-take scene in the Press Club in which her character, tipsy after a drinking session with the press reporter played by Mitchell, proposes marriage to him while making it clear to the audience that she is really in love with Stewart's Mr. Smith. Said Capra, "I defy any other actress to do that scene." Director Howard Hawks would later call it "one of the most beautiful love scenes I've ever seen in a picture."

DIFFICULTIES FOR JIMMY

Jimmy Stewart had his own special attitude toward the filming of "Mr. Smith." He realized instinctively that this was his great chance to become a major star, but he was anxious about it and took great care that nothing should happen to him before or during the shooting. He was aware that actors could be replaced, especially early in the filming, if they were injured or involved in scandal. He usually went directly home after the day's filming and stayed there until the next morning. Idiosyncratically, he would drive to the studio in an overly cautious manner, sometimes going so slowly that he enraged other motorists. On one occasion, he had to be cautioned by a policeman to keep moving.

Stewart became so intense about things going well that he decided to do something he had never done before on any of his previous films. He knew that Capra had a private screening room in his house, and he wrangled an invitation to see for himself how the day's shooting had gone. On his first visit to Capra's private movie room, he watched an hour and a half of film, showing take after take of the same scene from every conceivable angle and with every degree of lighting. He got so bored that he never went back.

Early on, the relationship between Stewart and Arthur on the set was cordial, pleasant, and professional. But as filming went on, it began to fray. Jean Arthur came to believe that Stewart was trying to upstage her by being overly arch and cute. She protested to Capra, but he was able to convince her that this was Stewart's normal acting style, and that it was important that Stewart's character portray naiveté and innocence. Stewart, for his part, found Arthur's histrionics before and after scenes offputting. Still, they made it work, and their scenes together were both effective and praiseworthy.

Stewart's great acting challenge came in the scenes in which he filibusters on the floor of the Senate Chamber—supposedly for more than several days. At the end of the oratorical marathon, Capra wanted him to be extremely hoarse, fighting to keep his voice audible. This is an almost impossible challenge for any actor, and Stewart was having only moderate success. Finally, Capra called in a throat specialist and said, "Doc, I know you are supposed to fix up throats, but can you ruin one?" The doctor replied affirmatively and twice a day he swabbed Stewart's throat with a mercury solution that swelled and irritated his vocal chords. It worked like a charm—and fortunately for movie history, it had no long-lasting effect on Stewart's distinctive voice.

Stewart and Arthur head for the set.

The Clock Problem

At one point when Capra was well into shooting the scene in the set of the Senate Chamber, Jim Preston, the expert on the Senate who had been hired to see that everything looked authentic, suddenly rushed onto the set. He yelled, "Stop it! Stop everything! Oh my God! It's all my fault! You'll have to throw it all away."

When Capra asked what the crisis was, Preston responded, "You can't use any of this film. I'll get the horselaugh at the Press Club. There's no *lock* on the clock!"

Once Capra calmed Preston down, he learned that a special lock had been put on the Senate clock to keep senators from opening it up to set it either backward or forward—so that a speech could go on longer or so they could adjourn early. Everyone, Preston said, knew about the lock and it was big enough to see from any vantage point in the chamber. Capra, fearing the loss of innumerable scenes already in the can, quickly made a deal with Preston. He would put a lock on the clock and reshoot several of the close-in scenes of the vice president at the rostrum. He even volunteered to make the lock oversized and in a contrasting dark

Capra and his stars at work on the set

color. Preston was apoplectic at this suggestion. "No! No! Don't you understand? It's gold! Gold!" In the end, Preston was pacified and the integrity of the Senate Chamber was preserved.

Shooting wrapped up on July 7, 1939—eight days over schedule and a quarter of a million dollars over budget.

"MR. SMITH" GOES BEFORE AN AUDIENCE

After an initial editing, "Mr. Smith" was previewed before a live audience in a local theater. It was customary for the director and his staff to be on hand for these events so that they could personally evaluate not just the

Capra and Stewart review a point in the script during filming.

overall reaction, but also how particular scenes were received by the viewers. This time, Capra decided not to go. He had come to believe that the people involved in the making of the film would be so invested in its success that they would be unable to clearly interpret audience reaction. Instead, he had his staff make an audiotape of audience reaction, as they watched the film. Then, in the quiet of his office, he listened to the tape as he watched a screening of the film. If he heard laughter, he knew a comic scene was successful. If, at a serious moment in the film, he heard coughing and the rustling of candy wrappers, he knew something was wrong with the scene. If there was absolute silence during an emotional scene, he knew it was having its effect.

As a result, Capra made a number of minor changes to "Mr. Smith," lengthening some scenes, curtailing others. He was perplexed at the audience reaction when Smith said he was "going up to Mount Vernon." Apparently, some in the audience knew that Mount Vernon was located

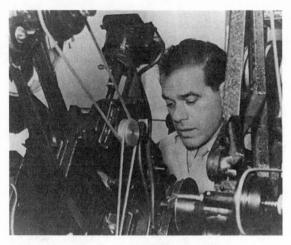

Capra in the editing room

a considerable distance south of the nation's capital. He decided it wasn't worth reshooting. He did, however, make one significant change. He noted that the audience's reaction peaked at the climax of Smith's eloquent and dramatic Senate speech, then drifted significantly when Smith returns to a hero's welcome in his hometown. As a result, Capra eliminated the entire last sequence and ended the film with Smith cradled in Saunders' arms after his collapse on the floor of the Senate Chamber.

PRAISE FROM THE CRITICS

Content that he now had the film where he wanted it, Capra made the decision to immediately screen it for the nation's film critics, a ritual that all directors and producers secretly dreaded. Capra and Columbia need not have worried. Following the screening, there was nothing but praise and good words for "Mr. Smith." Exuded *Variety*: "The most vital and stirring drama of contemporary American life yet told in films … superlative artistry." The *Los Angeles Times* was equally enthusiastic: "*Mr. Smith Goes to Washington* goes to town in probably the most hair-raising adventure along political, social, and patriotic lines ever conceived for the movies." Hedda Hopper, in her influential column, simply raved: "Not since Edison discovered motion pictures fifty years ago have we realized their possibilities until Frank Capra made *Mr. Smith Goes to Washington*. To me it is as great as the Gettysburg speech."

Emboldened by the early press praise, Columbia hurried up production of the movie trailer that would be shown in the nation's theaters prior to the film's actual appearance.

The ninety-second movie trailer for *Mr. Smith Goes to Washington* is a masterpiece of hyperbole. It opens with the statement, "This is the most important announcement this theater has ever made," after which distinguished commentator H. V. Kaltenborn narrates the trailer in sonorous tones, declaring the film to be "the most important, the most lively, the most significant film ever to come out of Hollywood." Frank Capra, who no doubt oversaw the production of the clip, makes two separate action appearances, as he is described as "the top director in Hollywood, the three-time winner of the distinguished Academy Awards, who again makes motion picture history." Additionally, his name is invoked four times by Kaltenborn and twice appears on the screen. The cast is declared to be the finest ever assembled. You can almost hear the film groan under the weight of its own self-importance.

Interestingly, the final seconds of the preview trailer show the parade in which Smith and Saunders are celebrated as hometown heroes. Since this ending was deleted from the movie itself, the trailer must have been made before the final editing of the film.

DISASTER AT THE PREMIERE

Most of the outdoor scenes, including Jefferson Smith's two sequences at the Lincoln Memorial, were filmed in the nation's capital. The city had for some time been abuzz about this Capra movie that would feature the workings of Congress. On the basis of the early reviews, the National Press Club sent Columbia a letter asking for "the privilege of sponsoring here the premier showing of your new picture *Mr. Smith Goes to Washington*.... We would plan to invite the newspaper people of Washington, all members of Congress, and other notables in official life."

It looked like a major coup. The opportunities for publicity from such an event seemed endless. Columbia eagerly accepted, and arrangements were made for what they were sure would be the movie premiere of a lifetime.

October 16, 1939, was officially declared "Mr. Smith" day in Washington. Politicians and celebrities came from as far as Boston to attend a special luncheon at the Press Club, which, in honor of the event, admitted women for the first time in its history. A military band saluted

Stewart's celebrated filibuster scene

the film with patriotic marches. Speeches from dignitaries lauded the film they had not yet seen. At a formal dinner that evening, Frank Capra and Harry Cohn were both saluted as visionaries and patriots. Later, limousines pulled up to Constitution Hall where Supreme Court justices, cabinet officers, senators, and generals shared space with an eager audience of more than four thousand special invitees. The vice president arrived to enthusiastic applause. Before the film started, Capra was introduced and stood up proudly as spotlights searched him out.

Then the movie started—and somewhere along the line, things started to go bad. There was murmuring in the crowd when the new senator Smith toured Washington and saw the Liberty Bell. Everyone there knew that the bell resided in Philadelphia. There was shuffling of feet and soft whispering when Smith said he was going "up to Mount Vernon." Suddenly, the voices on the screen began talking with fast, high-pitched voices: The film had jumped a sprocket wheel. Once that was restored, the audience became restive and people began talking over the film. When the plot of the film became clear and senators were portrayed as corrupt, someone yelled, "Outrage!" Another yelled, "Insult!" A couple got up and ostentatiously left the theater. Soon, others followed their lead. By the time the film concluded and "The End" appeared on the screen, the theater was more than half empty. A few people cautiously applauded, others softly booed. Later, at a "victory party" at the National Press Club, a gaggle of infuriated reporters, outraged at the way the Washington press had been portrayed in the film, confronted Capra to express their displeasure. The premiere that Columbia had expected would send their film skyrocketing into the marketplace had ended in a shambles.

Back in Hollywood, Capra and Cohn licked their wounds. The press follow-up did nothing to comfort them. Senator Alben Barkley was quoted as saying, "The picture is a grotesque distortion of the way the Senate is run, as grotesque as anything I have ever seen.... Imagine the vice president of the United States winking at a pretty girl in the balcony to encourage a filibuster. Can you visualize Jake Garner winking up at Hedy Lamar to egg her on?" Said another senator, "I speak for the whole body. The vote is 'no' and it is 96 to 0."

That was not the worst news. A letter arrived in Harry Cohn's office from Joseph P. Kennedy, the American ambassador in London. He had previewed the film and felt that it ridiculed democracy, that it would be a blow to the morale of our allies, and that it would be construed as propaganda favoring the Axis powers. He urged that the film never be distributed in Europe. Other Hollywood studios suggested to Columbia that it should not release "Mr. Smith" for fear that Congress would pass punitive legislation that could harm the entire movie industry.

The *Times-Herald* greets the film.

After much soul-searching and heated debate, Cohn and Capra decided to take the risk and release the film to the nation's theaters. They were still confident that it was a great film and that movie audiences would agree with them. In late November of 1939, *Mr. Smith Goes to Washington* went into national distribution.

Their confidence in the film was quickly vindicated. Local critics were uniformly laudatory: "It says all the things about America that have been crying out to be said—and says them beautifully"; "The high privilege of being an American citizen finds its best and most effective expression in *Mr. Smith Goes to Washington*"; "For the first time, the screen has become eloquent in relation to the significance of our times"; "Time after time, Mr. Capra stresses that only in America could one man fight this lone battle and win"; "There is a great movie at the Radio City Music Hall ... *Mr. Smith Goes to Washington*. Everyone should see it."

And audiences loved the film. It played well and long in theaters all across the country. Despite its high cost, "Mr. Smith" turned a profit on its first run.

HIGH EXPECTATIONS AT THE ACADEMY AWARDS

"Mr. Smith" was nominated by the Academy eleven times, including Outstanding Production (Columbia), Best Actor (Jimmy Stewart), Best Supporting Actor (Claude Rains), Best Director (Frank Capra), Best Original Story (Lewis Foster), and Best Screenplay (Sidney Buchanan). The Awards banquet was held on February 29, 1940, with Bob Hope handing out the Oscars. Capra and Cohn and their parties were in a celebratory mood, which quickly faded when, as the evening wore on, it became apparent that this was *Gone with the Wind*'s night. Oscar after Oscar went to Selznick's Civil War drama which virtually shut out all the other contenders. When the lights were finally raised in the hall, *Mr. Smith Goes to Washington* had received just one Oscar. It went to Lewis Foster for the Best Original Story of 1939.

That award made the purchase of Foster's novel one of the great bargains in movie history. Columbia had paid Foster just $1,500, and there is no record of anyone at Columbia ever buying him that lunch at the Brown Derby.

As it turned out, Ambassador Kennedy's strong reservations about "Mr. Smith's" effect on European audiences were completely wrong. Wherever it was permitted to play in war-torn Europe, it received critical acclaim and box office success. In 1942, the Nazi Party forbade the showing of all American films within thirty days. One French village with a single theater decided to take full advantage of that one month of freedom. It showed *Mr. Smith Goes to Washington* for thirty straight days.

After Mr. Smith Goes to Washington

Frank Capra left Harry Cohn and Columbia after "Mr. Smith" and formed his own production company, seeking the artistic freedom he had always craved. His first independent film was *Meet John Doe*, starring Gary Cooper and Barbara Stanwyck. It was a critical and financial success and won an Academy Award, but high federal wartime taxes and the approaching conflict convinced him to fold his enterprise.

Immediately after Pearl Harbor, Capra enlisted in the United States Army as a major and, as a member of General George Marshall's staff, he produced and directed eleven documentary films intended to boost American morale. Known as the "Why We Fight" series, they are regarded as masterpieces of patriotic propaganda.

After the war, Capra resumed his movie career and over the next fifteen years directed successful films, including *Arsenic and Old Lace*, *It's a Wonderful Life*, *A Hole in the Head*, and *Pocketful of Miracles*. Although many of these movies were highly regarded and financially successful, he never was able to fully recapture the magic of his earlier career. In 1982, the American Film Institute honored him with its AFI Lifetime Achievement Award. In all, Capra was nominated for six Academy Awards as Best Director and six times for Best Picture, and he won a total of six Oscars. In 1991, Capra died in his sleep at his home in La Jolla, California, at the age of ninety-four.

Harry Cohn continued as the head of Columbia Pictures until his death in 1958. In the two decades following "Mr. Smith," he produced such noteworthy films as *All the King's Men*, *Death of a Salesman*, *The Member of the Wedding*, *The Caine Mutiny*, *The Bridge on the River Kwai*, and *From Here to Eternity*. Despite the production of such highly regarded films, Cohn always retained an affection for his earlier two-reel movies and his lesser-known comedies. He kept "The Three Stooges" on Columbia's payroll long after their reign as comedy stars was over. Cohn's relationship with Capra ended in the 1940s, but he always recognized that Capra's films were the turning points in Columbia's fortunes. In 1989, his *Mr. Smith Goes to Washington* was added to the

United States National Film Registry as a "culturally, historically and aesthetically significant" film.

✻ ✻ ✻

Jimmy Stewart's role as "Mr. Smith" established him firmly in the top ranks of Hollywood stars. He immediately made a succession of successful films: *Destry Rides Again*, with Marlene Dietrich; *Made for Each Other*, with Carole Lombard; and *Shop around the Corner*, with Margaret Sullivan. In 1940, he won the Academy Award for his brilliant star turn in *Philadelphia Story*, which also featured Cary Grant and Katharine Hepburn. By this time, his slow and infectious drawl had became ingrained in the public consciousness and was already widely imitated by mimics and comedians, a form of flattery enjoyed by only a few other people in the public eye.

When World War II came, Stewart, already an experienced pilot, became the first movie star to enlist in the American armed forces. He joined the Army Air Corps and earned his commission as a second lieutenant just a month after Pearl Harbor. He went on to become one of the most decorated heroes of the war. As a bomber pilot with the 445 and 453 bombardment groups, he flew more than twenty missions over Nazi-occupied Europe, earning the admiration of both his comrades and his superiors.

He was twice decorated with the Distinguished Flying Cross for his actions in combat and was given the *Croix de*

The only surviving poster of the French showing of "Mr. Smith"

Guerre by the French. He also won the Air Medal with oak leaf clusters, and, after the war, he achieved the rank of brigadier general.

His first film after the war was Capra's *It's a Wonderful Life*, for which he was nominated for another Academy Award. For the next several decades, Stewart starred in dozens of heralded films, including *Winchester 73, The Far Country, The Glenn Miller Story*, and *Strategic Air Command*. A favorite actor of Alfred Hitchcock, Stewart was featured in a number of that director's finest films: *Rope, Rear Window, The Man Who Knew Too Much*, and *Vertigo*.

In his later life, Stewart became one of the most honored film actors of the twentieth century. He died in 1994, at the age of eighty-nine, having lived a life of celebrity and fame, a life that never seemed to have affected his personality or demeanor. As Harry Truman once said, "If Bess and I had been lucky enough to have had a son, I would have wanted him to be like Jimmy Stewart."

Jean Arthur continued her successful movie career after "Mr. Smith." So strong was her appeal to moviegoers and directors after that film that she became one of the finalists for the role of Scarlett O'Hara. Later that same year, she starred in *Only Angels Have Wings* with Cary Grant, and then went on to make other first-rate films with such stars as Robert Cummings, Ronald Colman, and John Wayne. In 1943, she was nominated for the Academy Award for her performance in *The More the Merrier*, and she remained Columbia's top star well into that decade. Eventually, her career became a victim to her shyness and stage fright. She left Columbia and turned down innumerable film offers that could have sustained her popularity. She did later star in two more films—Billy Wilder's *A Foreign Affair* and George Stevens' iconic *Shane*, in which she gave a brilliant performance as the valiant wife of a homesteader. In the mid-1950s, she abandoned Hollywood altogether and turned her attentions to the stage.

She scored major triumphs on Broadway in the revival of *Peter Pan* and *Joan of Arc*. But once again, stage fright overcame her and she left her role as St. Joan in mid-performance. In 1966, she attempted television, but "The Jean Arthur Show" was canceled by CBS after only twelve episodes. She did a brief teaching stint at Vassar College and at the North Carolina School of the Arts, where one of her most promising students was the then-unknown Meryl Streep.

In 1966, Jean Arthur returned to private life. She lived quietly, almost reclusively, in Carmel, California, where she died in 1991 at the age of ninety-two.

※ ※ ※

Lewis Foster continued working in Hollywood for more than two decades after "Mr. Smith," as a writer, a director, and a producer. He was involved in more than a dozen films and directed a number of successful television shows, including Disney's immensely popular "Zorro" series. At his death in 1974, he was saluted as a major contributor to American films, and he is remembered as the winner of his one Academy Award—for the original story of *Mr. Smith Goes to Washington*.

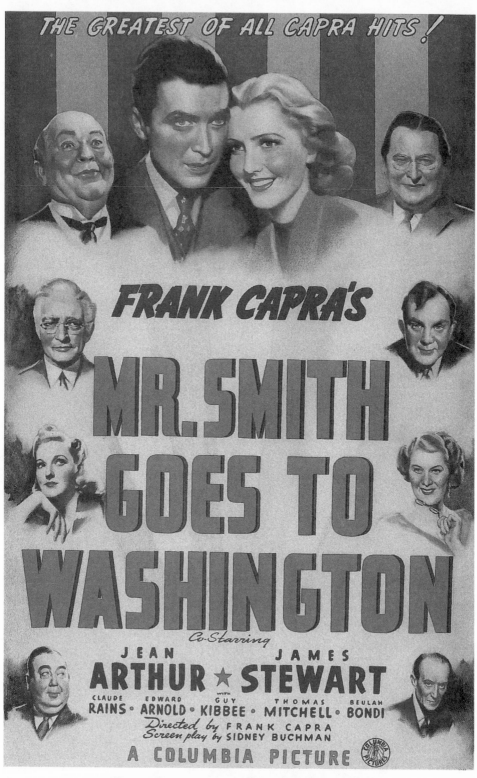

Poster for *Mr. Smith Goes to Washington*

MR. SMITH GOES TO WASHINGTON
THE FINAL FACTS

Studio:	Columbia Pictures
Producer:	Frank Capra
Director:	Frank Capra
Screenplay:	Sidney Buchman
Original Story:	Lewis R. Foster
Photographer:	Joseph Walker
Art Direction:	Lionel Banks
Release Date:	October 16, 1939
Running Time:	125 minutes
Cost of Production:	$1,500,000
Box Office (through 1985):	$3,860,000

Cast

Jefferson Smith................Jimmy Stewart
Clarissa Saunders.............Jean Arthur
Sen. Joseph Paine.............Claude Rains
Jim Taylor ....Edward Arnold
Gov. Hubert Hopper..........Guy Kibbee
Diz Moore.........................Thomas Mitchell
Chick McGann ....Eugene Pallette
Ma Smith...........................Beulah Bondi
President of Senate ....Harry Carey
Emma Hopper ....Ruth Donnelly
Bill Griffith ....William Demarest
Susan Paine......................Astrid Allwyn
Senator Agnew.................H. B. Warner

Awards

Academy Award Nominations: Best Director, Best Screenplay, Best Original Story, Best Actor, Best Supporting Actor, Best Art Direction, Best Score, Best Editing, Best Sound.

Academy Award Won: Lewis R. Foster for Best Original Story.

The Strand Magazine

THE HOUND OF
THE BASKERVILLES

THE STORY

The idea of creating a detective as the principal character in a novel had been rummaging around in Conan Doyle's brain for several years. He had already sketched out the personality and talents of his detective. He would be highly intellectual, physically strong, coldly analytical, musically inclined, and able to deduce truths out of clues that others could not see or understand. Now, he needed to give his detective hero a distinctive and memorable name—not just to make this one story interesting but because, if he could fulfill his dreams, it might be a name remembered in the decades ahead.

After much thought, he came up with the name he would use. He took his pen in hand and wrote it down

Sir Arthur Conan Doyle

firmly so that he would not misplace it or forget it. He would call his detective—Sherringford Holmes.

Conan Doyle's Early Start

It was important to Conan Doyle that this new story be a success. Even though he was first of all a physician and earned his living as Arthur Conan Doyle, M.D., he had developed a modest reputation as a writer. It was a reputation that had come slowly and had been hard won.

He had actually begun a literary career of sorts at an early age. The product of a dissolute father and a devoted mother who loved to tell stories, young Arthur inherited the mantle of storyteller himself with a ready-made audience: He had ten brothers and sisters.

Sent away from home for his education, he continued to entertain friends and fellow students with his rousing tales. He also proved to be a splendid athlete, excelling at a wide variety of sports. He practiced his writing skills with a lengthy daily letter to his mother and by writing poetry.

Even though he was inclined toward the arts, Arthur's practical streak influenced him toward medicine. He entered the medical school at the University of Edinburgh, where he made the acquaintance of future authors James Barrie and Robert Louis Stevenson, both of whom encouraged him to continue writing and telling stories. He also came under the tutelage on Dr. Joseph Bell, who dazzled Doyle with his talents for observation and diagnosis—and whose skills he would later remember in his own literary work.

Just two years into his medical studies, Conan Doyle wrote a short story called "The Mystery of Sasassa Valley," and his story was accepted by an Edinburgh publication called *Chandler's Journal*. His story earned him three guineas, but it was enough to convince him that there could be money in writing. Later that same year, still another of his stories, "The American Tale," was published in *London Society*.

During his educational years, Conan Doyle's life was enlivened by two dramatic ocean voyages—to the Arctic and to Africa—both times as a ship's medical officer. These were life-changing experiences that broadened his interest in the world and expanded his literary vision. As he said later, "They awakened the soul of a born wanderer." All his life, he would pursue his love of travel and adventure.

While earning his living as a practicing physician, Conan Doyle continued his avocation of writing stories on a wide variety of subjects: history, medicine, sports, and adventure. His work was published in British magazines and periodicals such as *Templar Bar, Boy's Own Paper,* and The *Illustrated London News,* and the payments augmented his modest income as a doctor.

All his life, he had been an avid and relentless reader of books and periodicals on a wide variety of subjects. Along the way, he became a devotee of Edgar Allan Poe, the American writer whose unusual, sometimes macabre, work had a profound influence on him. In 1841, in his story "The Gold Bug," Poe had created the word "detective" to describe a man who solves crimes by the use of clues and logic. The hero of this story solved a mystery through use of a cryptogram, but he was not what we think of as a "detective" today. However, in his next work, "Murders in the Rue Morgue," Poe gave the world the detective C. Auguste Dupin. Using what Poe described as "ratiocination," in which he combines deductive thinking with creative imagination, and putting himself into the mind of the criminal, Dupin solves a seemingly unsolvable crime. Poe wrote two other stories featuring his detective Dupin—"The Mystery of Marie Roget" and "The Purloined Letter." Thus, the modern detective was born.

Half a century later, in 1887, Conan Doyle decided to revisit his notes on the detective story that he was planning to write: "Ormand Sacker—from Afghanistan. Lived at 221B Baker St. with Sherringford Holmes—The laws of evidence. Reserved, sleepy-eyed young man—Philosopher—collector of rare violins. An Amateur...chemical laboratory...'I have four hundred a year—I am a consulting detective ...'"

Conan Doyle had also made a note to remember the diagnostic techniques of his old friend and mentor, Dr. Joseph Bell, under whom he had trained at the University of Edinburgh. Bell had an uncanny knack not just for diagnosing illness, but also for determining the circumstances and character of his patients. He taught Conan Doyle that the secret to "ratiocination" was constant learning, careful observation, and thoughtful deduction.

Conan Doyle at his writing desk

Conan Doyle had long planned to write his first novel. He realized that as an author of short stories he could never realize his full ambitions as a writer or make the money he needed to quit his medical practice. He had already sketched out his idea for the plot. The detective and his friend would meet and agree to share lodging in London at 221B Baker Street. The detective would be described as having a profound knowledge of chemistry, sensational literature, botany, and geology. There would be a murder, which the detective would solve through observation and deduction—involving a complex story of a forced marriage in the Mormon church in Utah, a revenge murder of the culprit in London by the use of poisoned tablets, and deductions by the hero detective that identify a London cabbie as the murderer. He would call his novel *A Tangled Skein*.

Conan Doyle wrote quickly and confidently, seldom making corrections or alterations. But as he began this novel, he found himself unhappy with the names he had given his principal characters. Ormand Sacker, the name he had given to his detective's friend and foil, sounded too unusual and difficult to remember. He ran some other possibilities through his mind, then recalled a man he greatly admired, a fellow physician in the South Sea and also a Scot: Dr. James Watson. Rather than duplicate the name and give offense, he settled on John Watson. And, yes, his character would also be a doctor, permitting Conan Doyle to utilize his medical knowledge during the writing of the story.

Then there was Sherringford Holmes. The name didn't seem quite right. After some brief thought, Doyle changed the name to Sherringford Hope. After writing that name several times in his tale, he had still another thought and changed it yet again; his detective would now bear the name Sherlock Holmes.

Conan Doyle finished his novel in three weeks. It had all the ingredients he had hoped for—murder, mystery, obscure clues, brilliant deductions, fascinating villains, and an ending that tied up all the loose ends. More important, he had created the detective he had hoped for—a man who was brilliant, arrogant, solitary in his ways, yet loyal to his friends, a careful student of detail, and capable of dazzling deductive reasoning. But he also made Holmes a flawed human being, dependent, when not mentally challenged, on a seven-and-a-

A traditional image of
Sherlock Holmes

half percent solution of heroin which he injects by needle. At one point, Conan Doyle had his detective describing to Watson what he feels is his mission in life: "There's the scarlet thread of murder running through the colourless skein of life, and our duty is to unravel it and isolate it, and expose every inch of it." He decided he liked the "scarlet" reference better than the "skein of life" reference—and so he changed the novel's title to *A Study in Scarlet*.

With his novel in hand, he faced the problems of publication. His reputation as a short story writer was no guarantee that *A Study in Scarlet* would find an automatic market. He first submitted the manuscript to *Cornhill Magazine*, only to find it rejected because of its awkward length. It was, the publisher said, too long for serialization but too short for separate publication as a book. Undeterred, Conan Doyle sent his story

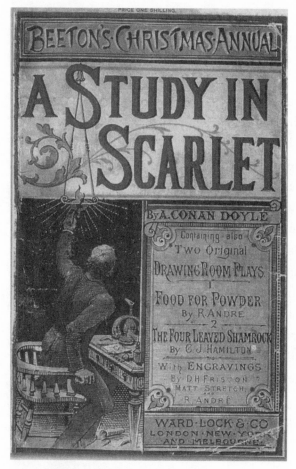

Beeton's **annual christmas issue**

off to a number of other publishers, but without favorable result. Some simply did not respond, and one sent the package back unopened. Finally, Doyle mailed it to Ward Lock & Co., a book agent with a reputation for sensational literature. The editor gave it to his wife, who was herself a novelist, and she saw the brilliance of the story. Ward Lock offered Conan Doyle twenty-five pounds for the copyright. Conan Doyle requested royalties instead but was refused. The disappointed author reluctantly accepted cash and agreed to its publication. The world was about to meet Sherlock Holmes.

However, the introduction of Sherlock Holmes would require a bit of a wait. Month after month, Conan Doyle waited for *A Study in Scarlet* to be published. Finally, in November of 1887, it made its appearance, not as a separate novel, but as part of a compendium called *Beeton's Christmas Annual*. Doyle's novel was one of three stories separated by some articles, puzzles, and comedic sketches. It was a disappointing debut for Sherlock Holmes, but this did not keep him from being noticed. The publication cost one shilling and sold out in a matter of days. *A Study in Scarlet* got a number of good reviews, one of which remarked that "the author showed genius" and that

Sherlock Holmes was "a character of promise." In fact, the reception of Holmes provoked enough interest that the publisher brought it out as a separate book the next year. Conan Doyle now had his own novel between its own covers, some critical acclaim from his peers, and a small income as a writer. But he was still dominated by his old life as a practicing physician.

For the next several years, Conan Doyle continued seeing his patients and visiting his writing table when he found the time. He wrote five more novels over the next two years and further established himself as a writer worth watching. Lock, sensing a continuing interest in Conan Doyle's detective, commissioned him to write another Sherlock Holmes novel. In 1890, Conan Doyle responded with *The Sign of Four*, a complex tale involving murder, treasure, a backstory of intrigue in India, and death by blow dart. More important, it fleshed out the character of Sherlock Holmes and his relationship with John Watson.

Readers now had a clear image of Holmes: "rather over six feet," "excessively thin," "eyes sharp and piercing," "hawk-like nose," "hands of extreme delicacy." And readers were becoming more familiar with Holmes' habits and idiosyncrasies—playing his violin, smoking his pipe, fiddling with his chemical equipment, looking through his magnifying glass, and stalking his room in thought. They knew he was a master of disguise, a patriot and admirer of Queen Victoria, and a man of boundless physical and mental energy. They knew he had an affectionate but adversarial relationship with the police and Scotland Yard. And, most important, they became fascinated by his ability to search out facts and events from the most obscure of clues.

They had also come to know and like Dr. Watson, his amiable, frequently befuddled, but always helpful and faithful friend. They knew that Watson had a military background, that he was capable and brave, but that he was too guileless to be a detective himself. They knew that Watson was not only a confidant of Holmes but also his fierce defender. And they knew that Watson was extremely literate— because it was he who had recorded and chronicled Sherlock Holmes' cases so brilliantly and so entertainingly.

Watson and Holmes in the original drawings

The demand for additional Holmes stories grew, and Conan Doyle answered the demand with a series of short stories that were individually published over the next several years in the *Strand Magazine*. From July 1891 to June 1892, readers got a full dose of their new hero. Altogether, twelve stories were published by the *Strand Magazine*. The titles alone are enough to given anyone the flavor of these fascinating and exotic mysteries: "A Scandal in Bohemia," "The Red-Headed League," "The Bascombe Valley Mystery," "Five Orange Pips," "The Twisted Lip," "The Blue Carbunkle," "The Speckled Band," and "The Beryl Coronet." Doyle was giving his readers exactly what they wanted—bizarre plots, exotic settings, baffling clues, and, of course, magnificent sleuthing by Holmes. Later in 1892, the twelve stories were collected together and published as a book entitled *The*

Adventures of Sherlock Holmes. It was published in England, Canada, and the United States, and it was translated into French, German, and Italian. Sherlock Holmes had become a true international star.

Conan Doyle began turning Sherlock Holmes stories out at a rate of one a month. While he was wearying of his detective, he realized that Holmes had become a real moneymaker and would enable him to a gradually wind down his medical practice so that he could concentrate entirely on writing. Conan Doyle was remarkably prolific. At the same time that he was creating his Holmes stories, he continued to write other novels and short stories, but he seemed to have less and less time for what he considered his more important work. Sherlock Holmes was getting in his way.

THE END OF HOLMES

Within just another year, Conan Doyle had produced twelve more Holmes stories, collected under the title *The Memoirs of Sherlock Holmes*, with such intriguing tales as "The Yellow Faces," "The Musgrave Ritual," and "The Reigate Puzzle." He called the last story of this series "The Final Problem"—and for good reason. Conan Doyle by now had decided he had to get rid of Sherlock Holmes, and he dispatched him in dramatic fashion. He had Holmes track his arch-enemy, Professor Moriarty, to Switzerland, where Holmes encounters Moriarty on a path overlooking the treacherous Reichenbach Falls. Locked in mortal combat, the two slip and plunge to their deaths on the rocks below.

When "The Final Problem" appeared in the *Strand Magazine*, there was a public uproar that amazed Conan Doyle and bewildered the magazine's publishers. Readers, many of whom had come to accept both Holmes and Watson as real-life, flesh-and-blood characters, were distraught at Holmes' demise. More than twenty thousand people indignantly canceled their subscriptions to the *Strand Magazine*. Abusive mail began arriving at the magazine's offices demanding Holmes' return. But Conan Doyle was undeterred, and his readers would have a long wait.

Conan Doyle was certain that he was now through with Sherlock Holmes. He happily turned his attentions to more serious literary

Holmes and Moriarty at Reichenbach Falls

endeavors for which he was sure destiny intended him. For the next eight years, he did his best to avoid his now-celebrated detective, despite the demands of publishers and readers. Between 1893 and 1902, he turned out a dozen novels, a host of short stories, and innumerable treatises on a wide variety of subjects. He also authored a monumental work on the Boer War that was instrumental in his winning a knight bachelorhood from King Edward VII.

THE RETURN OF HOLMES

In March of 1901, Conan Doyle joined a friend on a golfing vacation in Norfolk. During the four days that he spent relaxing in the area, he heard folktales and legends of nearby Dartmoor and its deadly quicksands and bogs. It was said that spectral hounds inhabited the area, including one huge, black hellhound with red eyes that brought certain death to all who saw it. The setting and the story of the hound captured his imagination and set his creative gears into motion. On the carriage ride back to the train, he asked the driver his name. Replied the driver, "Baskerville, sir."

Back at his writing table, Conan Doyle quickly concluded that if he wrote a story based on the legends of the hound and the moor it would have to be a mystery and that it would require a detective to unravel its complexities. He also knew that if the detective were not Sherlock Holmes, his publisher would be disappointed and his readers would be heartbroken. He had already killed off Holmes in "The Final Problem," but that was a dilemma easily solved. He would simply backdate the time of this story and have Watson describe it as having taken place prior to the incident at Reichenbach Falls.

Conan Doyle began to fill out the details of the story he had in mind. The title almost wrote itself: *The Hound of the Baskervilles*. There would be an aristocratic and hereditary family surnamed Baskerville, living in Dartmoor in Devonshire in their ancestral home called Baskerville Hall.

Holmes and Watson, holed up in their residence at 221B Baker Street, would be informed of the death of the head of the family and of the legend of a great hound that might be responsible for the death. Holmes would send Watson to Devonshire to report back to him, while Holmes would disguise himself and prowl the countryside and the moor, which Doyle would call "The Grimpen Mire," in search of clues. The new head of the family, visiting from America, would make an appearance and would serve as the central character in the dangerous environment of the hall and the moor. There would be several threatening characters lurking about Baskerville Hall to complicate the picture, and possibly a hint of romance between the new heir and a lady in a neighboring house. There would be a dramatic climax involving the legendary hound and the Baskerville heir—and Holmes would save the heir and reveal the identity of the real killer, detailing the clues that led him to the solution.

Conan Doyle wrote with his customary speed and precision, rarely making a false start or needing to make extensive changes. Within

The Hound

a matter of months, he sent his novel off to the *Strand Magazine* for serialization. The news that Sherlock Holmes was returning after almost a decade created genuine excitement in the literary world. When the first episode was published in August of 1901, there was a queue outside the *Strand* offices that stretched around the building and out into the street. Bribes were offered for prepublication copies. Almost overnight, subscriptions to the *Strand Magazine* grew by more than thirty thousand. Within a matter of months, the issue with the first "Hound" installment was in its seventh printing. Sherlock Holmes was back!

Following its serialization in the *Strand Magazine*, *The Hound of the Baskervilles* was published the next year as a self-contained novel and became a huge success in both England and America. With Sherlock Holmes' following soaring to new heights, it was only a matter of time before he would leap off the printed page and materialize before a live audience. This happened in 1899, when the American actor William

Gillette wrote and starred in a Holmesian drama entitled simply *Sherlock Holmes*. His play opened to great acclaim in New York, toured America for more than a year, and then moved to England where it was heralded by cheering audiences. The show played an extended stay in London and in 1902 gave a royal command performance before the king and queen. William Gillette was a picture-perfect Holmes in appearance and he inspired future illustrators trying to capture the detective's pictorial persona. Gillette introduced the phrase, "Elementary, my dear Watson," which had never appeared in any of the original stories. Booth Tarkington, after witnessing one of the Gillette's performances, told him, "I would rather watch you play Sherlock Holmes than be a child again on Christmas morning."

SHERLOCK HOLMES GOES TO THE MOVIES

In the early twentieth century, a new and startling medium became available to present Sherlock Holmes to his adoring public: motion pictures.

The first attempts were brief and forgettable, and, oddly, they were not British. The very first Holmes film was made by an American film company in 1903. Titled "Sherlock Holmes Baffled," it lasted only a few minutes and had no discernible plot. Over the next decade, primitive attempts at Holmes movies were made in Italy, Denmark, Germany, and France, and it was not until 1917 that the British film industry undertook its own attempt at presenting the great detective. From the outset, however, it was clear that Sherlock Holmes and the Conan Doyle stories made excellent movie material—and that *The Hound of the Baskervilles* was a natural for portraying on-screen magic.

The first British movie production of "Hound" was made in 1921 by Stoll Pictures. It was part of a series of fifteen Holmes films and starred a well-known actor, Eille Norwood, in the lead role. A noble effort, it nevertheless failed to convey the mystery and suspense of the novel. A London townhouse sufficed as Baskerville Hall and a misty park substituted for the Grimpen Mire.

The next film effort to capture the "Hound" tale came with the advent of talking pictures in 1932, when Britain's Gainsborough

William Gillette

Pictures selected actor Robert Rendel to take on the Holmes role. Despite some good production values and lighting techniques, Holmes enthusiasts were generally disappointed. Fascinated with the idea of sound, the film was heavy on dialogue and short on action. The Baskerville legend was presented as a prologue rather than in an action sequence, and Robert Rendell did not live up to viewers' preconceptions of how the detective should look. As one reviewer said, "Rendell acts well but he's not Holmes." It would be seven more years before the right actor came along.

THE COCKTAIL CHAT THAT REINVENTED HOLMES

In the Hollywood world of the late 1930s, a great deal of business was conducted informally and among friends at private gatherings. There were a number of legendary hosts of the period, including the David O. Selznicks, George Cukor, Charlie Chaplin, and Louis B. Mayer. Marion Davies, actress and companion to William Hearst, was famous for her dazzling parties at her Santa Monica beach chalet.

It was at one of these Hollywood gatherings in 1937 that producers Darryl Zanuck and Gene Markey and director and actor Gregory Ratoff pulled aside to chat privately about their current movie projects. Zanuck was shepherding a number of films through Twentieth Century Fox, including *In Old Chicago* and *Alexander's Ragtime Band*. Ratoff was in the process of directing the film *Lancer Spy* and acting in *Seventh Heaven*. Markey was currently working on the script for *On the Avenue*, which would star Myrna Loy and Dick Powell. After trading comments on their films and indulging in some Hollywood gossip, they turned to the possibility of new movie properties. Markey, always looking for another assignment, said, "Somebody should do one of those damned Sherlock Holmes stories. It's been a long time." Zanuck agreed, but asked, "Who would you get to play Holmes?" Then they said, almost in unison because the answer was so obvious, "Basil Rathbone!"

THE PERFECT HOLMES

He was born Philip St. John Basil Rathbone in Johannesburg, South Africa, in 1892. When he was just three years of age, his father was accused of spying for the British government and the family fled to England. Rathbone was educated at Repton School in Devonshire, where he found at an early age that he liked being in school pageants and plays. After an amateur acting career, he made his first professional appearance in the Theatre Royal as Hortensio in Shakespeare's *The Taming of the Shrew*, and just a year later he traveled to America with an acting troupe, where he played a variety of Shakespearean roles. Rathbone returned to England an experienced and respected stage actor, but his career was interrupted by World War I.

Rathbone enlisted in the London Scottish Regiment, where he served alongside future acting stars Claude Rains, Herbert Marshall, and Ronald Colman. He distinguished himself throughout the conflict as an intelligence officer, displaying unusual courage in going behind enemy lines to secure information. For his valor, he was awarded the British Military Cross.

Following the war, Rathbone resumed his acting career, specializing again in Shakespearean roles. He performed on stages all over England and America during the 1920s, frequently with celebrated actors like Ethel Barrymore and Katharine Cornell. Rathbone was an impressive presence on stage; he was tall and well-proportioned, and he was graced with a sonorous speaking voice and an impressive, cultured English accent. It was only a matter of time before he got a call from the movie industry.

In 1925, Rathbone starred in a silent film called *The Masked Bride*, alongside such established movie performers as Mae Murray

Basil Rathbone

and Francis X. Bushman. Rathbone played the "heavy" in the film, a role that he seemed suited for, given his angular, hawk-nosed, strong-featured face. It was the first of a number of movie roles in which he appeared as a suave villain or a treacherous fiend. In 1935 alone, Rathbone was the abusive stepfather in *David Copperfield*, the distant husband in *Anna Karenina*, the cruel Pontius Pilate in *The Last Days of Pompeii*, and the evil Marquis St. Evremonde in *A Tale of Two Cities*. In all of these films, Rathbone's dramatic presence and knife-like face seemed to dominate the screen. The actress Mrs. Patrick Campbell would later describe the Rathbone visage as "two profiles pasted together."

By late 1938, the powers at Twentieth Century Fox had made their definite decision to produce a new Sherlock Holmes film. Their decision was made somewhat easier by the fact that the Conan Doyle stories were in the public domain and it would not be necessary to pay for film rights. Gene Markey was assigned to the project as producer and, after consulting with screenwriter Ernest Pascal, he decided on *The Hound of the Baskervilles* as the best vehicle. This was a story that had mystery, suspense, and an eerie setting that could be easily reproduced on film. Markey selected veteran Sidney Lanfield to direct and ordered Pascal and Lanfield to work together in adapting "Hound" for the screen. And he was steadfast on who would play Sherlock Holmes in his movie.

Because his appearance seemed to match so closely the drawings of Sherlock Holmes, created by Sydney Padget for the original Holmes stories—and because he had the accent, the intelligence, and the commanding presence to play the role—everyone at Twentieth Century agreed that Basil Rathbone was the ideal choice to portray Sherlock Holmes. Rathbone was currently at work on *The Adventures of Robin Hood*, playing the role of Sir Guy of Gisboune, but that film would be wrapped up by the time the Holmes script was finished and approved.

The role of Dr. Watson was just as easily filled. Nigel Bruce was available and under contract, and he seemed to fit the requirement of Watson perfectly. British to the core, he was accustomed to portraying characters who were avuncular and affable, and emanated a kind of endearing, fumbling charm. Though three years younger than Rathbone, Bruce would have little trouble portraying a senior role. The role of the romantic hero, the Baskerville heir, went to Richard Greene, a handsome leading man who had earlier starred in four successful films for Fox. The role of his romantic interest, Beryl Stapleton, was assigned to Wendy Barrie, a beautiful and talented English actress who had appeared in a number of British films. John Carradine, whose gaunt looks and threatening demeanor were already known to filmgoers, was tabbed to play the Baskerville Hall butler.

By late fall of 1938, the screenplay for "Hound" had been drafted, critiqued, revised, and finally signed off on by Markey. It was as faithful to Conan Doyle's original work as they could manage, given the technical and time restraints of a motion picture.

THE MOVIE SCRIPT FOR
THE HOUND OF THE BASKERVILLES

A man is seen running in a panic through the fog over a darkened moor. A terrifying howl, sounding as if it came from a great beast of some sort, is heard. The man falls to the ground and dies. There is a formal inquest into the death of the man, Sir Charles Baskerville, and it is concluded that he died of a heart attack. One of the inquest members, Mr. Frankland, disagrees and suggests that he was murdered and that the truth is being suppressed.

The scene changes to 221B Baker Street where Sherlock Holmes and Watson are in residence. Mrs. Hudson announces that a gentleman

Rathbone as Holmes

caller has left his cane. Holmes amazes Watson by deducing the character of the caller from his cane. The caller returns and introduces himself as Dr. Mortimer and informs Holmes of the death of Sir Charles and of his worries about his heir as the next victim. Holmes is told of the legend of the great hound that stalks the moor and is said to have killed a number of prior Baskerville family members, including the evil Sir Hugo Baskerville. He is told of the giant footprints found near Sir Charles' body and learns of an ancient curse.

Dr. Mortimer reads a description of the origin of the hound and the curse. There is a flashback scene in which Sir Hugo, two centuries earlier, is seen at Baskerville Hall, reveling with friends. He falls in love with a yeoman's daughter and imprisons her in his bedchamber. She escapes and a drunken Sir Hugo pursues her out over the moor. Later he and the girl are found dead. She has died from fatigue and terror, and Sir Hugo has been killed by a giant spectral hound which is seen standing over his body.

Dr. Mortimer meets Henry Baskerville, the new heir, at the dock after his journey from Canada. On the way to his hotel, a rock is thrown through the carriage window with a note on it warning him to stay away from Baskerville Hall, the ancestral home of the family.

Back at the Holmes flat, Dr. Mortimer informs the detective of the incident. Later Holmes learns from Sir Henry himself that one of his boots was stolen on the boat trip from Canada. Holmes and Watson follow their two visitors out onto the street, where an attempt on Sir Henry's life is averted by Holmes. The culprit escapes. At Sir Henry's hotel room, they discover that the stolen boot has been returned but that an old hunting boot has now been stolen. Holmes has traced the driver of the cab from near where the assassination attempt

Holmes hears the sound of the Hound.

took place. The driver informs Holmes that his passenger said his name was Sherlock Holmes. Sir Henry announces his determination to go to Baskerville Hall despite the danger. Holmes asks Watson to accompany Sir Henry while he, Holmes, stays in London.

At Baskerville Hall, Watson and Sir Henry meet the servants, a suspicious-looking couple named Barryman. During the night, Watson and Sir Henry hear disturbing baying sounds of a hound. Watson reports by letter to Holmes. The next day, Watson and Sir Henry meet a charming man named John Stapleton, who is accompanied by his beautiful stepsister, Beryl. It is obvious that Sir Henry is attracted to Beryl. They accept the Stapletons' dinner invitation for the following evening. At that dinner, Dr. Mortimer's wife performs a séance and tries to communicate with the departed spirit of Sir Charles. Her séance is interrupted by howling on the moor.

Sir Henry initiates a courtship of Beryl one day as they ride horses together on the moors. Their ride is interrupted by Watson and then the three of them are waylaid by an old geezer who tries to sell them various objects. As the man leaves their presence, Watson notes that he is limping on the opposite leg than that with which he approached them. Still later, Watson finds an unsigned note in his room requesting a meeting in a cave located in the moors. Out of curiosity, Watson keeps the rendezvous but takes the precaution of carrying a gun. The man who meets him is the same old codger he encountered earlier on the moors. After some verbal exchanges, the old man takes off his disguise and reveals himself to be Sherlock Holmes. Holmes explains that the reason for his play-acting is that it has allowed him to roam freely around the Grimpen Mire and study Baskerville Hall. He also tells Watson he is close to solving the crime.

While out on the moor, the two witness from a distance a huge hound attacking a man at the edge of a cliff. The man falls to his death on the rocks below. Holmes and Watson assume it must be Sir Henry, but they find that it is someone dressed in Sir Henry's clothing. Holmes recognizes him as a scruffy man he saw earlier near Baskerville Hall and identifies him as a wanted criminal known as "The Notting Hill Murderer."

Later, at Baskerville Hall, Holmes declares that the dead man must have been the killer of Sir Charles, that the case is solved, and that he and Watson are returning to London. Sir Henry and Beryl announce that they are in love and will be married. Holmes and Watson leave on the train, but the detective reveals then that Sir Henry's life is still at risk and that they will return to find the real killer.

After a dinner celebrating the coming nuptials, Sir Henry decides to walk back to Baskerville Hall alone across the moor. The carriage carrying Holmes and Watson back across the moor breaks down and they are forced to continue on foot.

At the Stapleton residence, John Stapleton says good night to Beryl, puts on a pair of gloves, and takes out the boot he has stolen

Holmes and Watson in *The Hound of the Baskervilles*

from Sir Henry. He goes out onto the moor to a secret cave where he keeps a large vicious hound. He shows the boot to the beast and then releases him to attack Sir Henry. The hound mounts a vicious assault on the Baskerville heir, but Holmes and Watson arrive in time to save him as they shoot the dog dead. While Watson carries the wounded victim back to Baskerville Hall, Holmes goes to investigate the pit in which the hound was kept. When he enters, Stapleton locks him in, but Holmes manages to find a tunnel and escapes.

Back at Baskerville Hall, Watson attends to Sir Henry's wounds. Stapleton attempts to poison Sir Henry, but Holmes arrives in time to intervene. Holmes then explains to everyone that Stapleton is the real killer and that his visage reveals him to be a Baskerville and a descendant of Sir Hugo, whose portrait hangs on the wall. Holmes explains that, as the next heir after Sir Henry, he would inherit if Sir Henry died, and that Stapleton had taken advantage of the legend of the hound to achieve his ends. The man known as "The Notting Hill Murderer" was, in fact, Mrs. Barryman's brother, who had been given Sir Henry's clothes and was then the accidental victim of the hound. Revealed as the murderer of various Baskervilles, Stapleton flees, but Holmes announces that constables have been stationed about the moor to apprehend him. Holmes is thanked by the family for his great detective work. As Holmes and Watson depart, Holmes turns to his friend and says, "Oh, Watson, the needle."

THE END

While the script was faithful in plot and spirit to the original story, a number of changes were made in order to present it effectively on the screen. The character called "Laura Lyons" in the novel, the daughter

Holmes ponders the Baskerville legend.

of the local litigator who is disowned by her father, was eliminated. The romance between Sir Henry and Beryl Stapleton was enhanced in the belief that this would appeal to viewers—and Beryl becomes Stapleton's stepsister instead of his wife in order to make the romance more acceptable.

The name of the Baskerville butler in the novel is "Barrymore." Scriptwriter Pascal, in deference to the famous acting family, changed it to "Barryman." Dr. Mortimer, who was a bachelor in the novel, was given a wife, and Mrs. Mortimer plays a key role in the suspense of the film. At the end, Stapleton flees the house after being exposed by Holmes. In the novel, he perishes in the quicksand of the moor.

SHERLOCK HOLMES COMES TO FOX

In order to film "Hound" in a limited amount of time, the studio constructed a massive set that spread over several acres on the back lot at Fox. It included the Holmes flat on Baker Street, the interiors of Baskerville Hall, the Stapleton residence, the cave in which Holmes conceals himself, the pit where the hound is kept captive and, most important, the vast, mysterious, fog-shrouded Grimpen Mire.

Shooting got under way in September of 1938 and it turned out to be a more complicated task than Fox had imagined. To begin with, the set for the moor was so extensive, so packed with man-made rocks, bluffs, cliffs, paths, and twists and turns that actors frequently became disoriented and missed their marks when filming began. Richard Greene, playing Sir Henry, once got completely lost and had to yell for help before he could retrace his steps. Craftsman were constantly repairing damage to the set and checking it for safety. Another problem was the machines that pumped out the fog for scenes on the moor. The original machines were far too effective, frequently clouding the scene and making the actors difficult to see. These were scrapped at a cost of $20,000 and new, lighter, less effusive equipment was brought in to take their place. Cameramen also found it difficult to move their heavy equipment around in the set as they changed from one scene to another.

Sometime during the filming of *The Hound of the Baskervilles*, Basil Rathbone discovered that he would not receive top billing in the film. The producer decided that should go to Richard Greene, who played the

The flashback sequence

handsome Sir Henry. Apparently, it did not strike Markey as odd that the man playing Sherlock Holmes in a Sherlock Holmes film should not be the star. There is no record of any objection to this on Rathbone's part, so it can be assumed that he accepted it with equanimity as a professional just doing the job he was hired to do.

The part of the Hound was given to a 140-pound Great Dane called Blitzen. The dog was a trained actor, part of the stable of animals owned by Carl Spity, who provided dogs for a number of Fox films—including Toto for *The Wizard of Oz* and Buck for *The Call of the Wild*. The name "Blitzen" was deemed inappropriate by the director because he thought it would call to mind an image of a gentle and beloved reindeer, rather than the fierce, wild, dangerous creature portrayed in the story. So, he blithely changed Blitzen's name to "Chief" for the official credits at the end of the film. Blitzen, a.k.a. Chief, spent just two days on the set and behaved and acted like the professional he was. Blitzen's owner was paid $125 for Blitzen's efforts.

To further complicate an already complicated filming, Pascal continued to revise the dialogue throughout the shooting. This was not unusual, as most film writers toyed with their scripts continuously as they developed new ideas or witnessed awkward moments in scenes. Of course, there always comes a moment of no return, and the last script change was made as late as February of 1939.

One casting problem remained—who should play the role of Sir Hugo in the flashback scenes. Logically, it should have gone to Morton Lowry, who played John Stapleton, because it was Stapleton's ancestor's portrait on the wall that helps Holmes deduce the identity of the killer. However, director Sidney Lanfield was afraid that if Lowry's face was obvious on the painting it would tip off the audience. The role instead went to Richard Greene, even though later Sir Hugo's portrait did look more like Morton Lowry than Greene.

Problems in the Cutting Room

When shooting finally wrapped up, film editor Robert Simpson saw some problems and called in director Lanfield. There is a scene near

Watson and Sir Henry on the trail of the Hound

the beginning of the film in which Mrs. Mortimer suggests to Dr. Mortimer that he take his concerns about the possible murder of Sir Charles to a detective named Sherlock Holmes. She then makes a lengthy explanation to Mortimer as to who the detective is and the cases he has solved. It was Simpson's opinion that this passage was completely gratuitous and that it slowed down the start of the film. Surely, thought Simpson, everyone in the audience would know who Sherlock Holmes was, and so the scene wound up on the cutting room floor. Simpson and Lanfield made other cuts. A scene in which Dr. Watson offers to leave the Holmes flat after Dr. Mortimer arrives was excised. A scene in which Stapleton finds Beryl and Sir Henry kissing was also taken out. There were some obvious discrepancies at various points in the film that worried the director and the editor. The Holmes flat was unlike anything described in the Conan Doyle novel. It looked like a luxury hotel suite, and its massive curved staircase was more befitting a mansion. On the screen, Baskerville Hall looked very much like the painted set it actually was. On the moor, Holmes uses a flashlight, a device not invented until a decade after the time in which *The Hound of the Baskervilles* is set. It was finally decided that each of these problems would probably be overlooked by theater audiences.

In order to make sure that viewers understood that the flashback scenes were events that happened long ago, a periphery of the written curse was added to the edges of the scenes. There was concern that the Hound, despite Blitzen's best efforts, did not look menacing enough. Conan Doyle had described him as "an enormous coal-black hound ... fire burst from its open mouth, its eye glowed with a smoldering glare, its muzzle and hackles and dewlap were outlines in flickering flame." What they had on the screen was a great big dog that snarled occasionally. They considered adding a luminous glow about the dog, as had been done in an earlier film, but this presented certain dangers to the existing footage and could require some reshooting. They eventually concluded that their Hound was fierce enough.

When the film was at last assembled, both the editor and the director noted that in all the suspenseful scenes on the moor—and they are extensive—no background music had been provided by David

Buttolph, the composer in charge of the film's music. They both agreed that the moor scenes would be far more moving if they were supported by appropriate mood music. But Buttolph had already completed his score and the recording session with the orchestra had been held days earlier. The expense of reconvening the musicians for another recording would simply be too high. And so, Holmes and Watson were permitted to prowl the mysterious Grimpen Mire in relative silence, with only their dialogue to stir the emotions of the audience.

There were other problems. The romance between Sir Henry and Beryl Stapleton was too cursory and weakly motivated, and it seemed to have blossomed almost overnight. The wounds to Sir Henry after his vicious attack by the Hound looked more like minor scratches. Part of the set that had looked impressive during filming looked like a dime-store version of Stonehenge on the screen. Reluctantly, they concluded that there was no time or money to reshoot scenes and that "Hound" would have to be sent out into the world with all its little sins and imperfections. Simpson eventually edited the film down to eighty-two minutes, a good ten minutes shorter than the standard length of contemporary films. The executives at Fox knew that theater owners would not be displeased.

When the minute-and-a-half trailer was sent out to the theaters in mid-March, Rathbone and Bruce discovered that they were now billed third and fourth—even though the trailer featured scenes with Holmes and Watson. It was the first and last time that actors playing Sherlock Holmes and Dr. Watson would receive such poor billing.

"HOUND" WINS OVER ITS AUDIENCE

The Hound of the Baskervilles opened nationwide on the weekend of March 31, 1939. The critics were almost unanimous in their praise. Said Frank Nugent of The *New York Times*, "The film succeeds rather well in reproducing Sir Arthur's macabre detective story along forthright cinema lines. The technicians have whipped up a moor at least twice as desolate as any ghost-story moor has need to be. The mist swirls steadily, the savage sound of the Baskerville hound is heard at all the appropriate moments …" One British reviewer remarked, "The Americans have done right by Conan Doyle." Another said simply, "It is a grand Sherlock Holmes!"

Bruce, Rathbone, and the director on set

The movie was a box office hit in America, and later in England and Europe. It was, in fact, one of the most successful and profitable movies released in 1939, a year that had more than its full share of great films. Fox realized immediately how to respond to such a moneymaking proposition: They hurried a second Sherlock Holmes film into production right away. Called *The Adventures of Sherlock Holmes*, it also starred Rathbone and Nigel Bruce in the key roles and was based on William Gillette's successful play script. It was also well received and made money for Fox.

As of this writing, there have been 217 Sherlock Holmes movies made, featuring seventy-six different actors playing the great detective. Every Holmes story written by Conan Doyle has been interpreted on the screen, and dozens have been made with newly contrived plots.

The Guinness Book of Records lists Sherlock Holmes as the "most portrayed character in film history." There have now been twenty-eight different film versions of "Hound" alone. And yet 1939's *The Hound of the Baskervilles* stands as the milestone movie of the genre. It was the progenitor of a series of Holmes films that has entertained generations of theatergoers. It proved to be a truly memorable film to everyone who saw it and it established an image of the great detective that lives on to this day.

**Blitzen, as the Hound,
on the attack**

AFTER THE HOUND OF THE BASKERVILLES

Sir Arthur Conan Doyle, after the remarkable success of "Hound," continued to do his best to divorce himself from Sherlock Holmes, but it was a fruitless task. He continued to write novels and stories on a wide variety of subjects, but the demands of his reading public for more of Holmes proved overpowering. In 1902, he received an offer from *Collier's Weekly* in America for twenty-five thousand pounds for a new series of Holmes stories. At about the same time, the *Strand Magazine* in London offered him one hundred pounds for every thousand words of new Holmes material. The offers, taken together, represented the greatest advance sum ever offered an author. Both offers came with a caveat: They insisted that the new Sherlock Holmes stories not be retrospective, like "Hound." Like Conan Doyle's readers, the magazine editors wanted the great detective brought back to life. The offer proved irresistible, the stipulation challenging. In his 1893 story, "The Final Problem," Conan Doyle had dispatched Holmes with seeming finality—a great fall from a high cliff onto the rocks below and a surging river to carry off the body. But Conan Doyle, as usual, was up to the task. He contrived an elaborate backstory in which Holmes did not actually fall, but had instead left a deceptive note for Watson so that he could prowl the world in search of wisdom without his enemies pursuing him. Conan Doyle's readers docilely accepted the absurd premise and read eagerly on.

Conan Doyle wrote thirteen new Holmes tales and assembled them under the banner *The Return of Sherlock Holmes*. The author invented more intriguing titles, such as "The Dancing Men," "The Adventure of the Golden Pince-Nez," "The Second Stain," and "The Six Napoleons." They were just what readers on both sides of the Atlantic wanted—tales with suspense, exotic settings, and brilliant deductions. In Britain, customers lined up outside newsstands and bookstores, pushing and shoving to get the latest installments. When the stories were published in the United States, an initial press run of thirty thousand copies sold out almost immediately and another twenty-eight thousand were added to the run.

Conan Doyle once again tried to separate himself from Holmes, fearing that he would be remembered not for his more serious work but for what he considered his less important detective stories. He lived almost another three decades without seemingly taking up his pen on Holmes' behalf. Yet, after his passing in 1930, two additional Holmes stories were published. It would seem that, in life as in fiction, Sherlock Holmes had the last word.

✻ ✻ ✻

Basil Rathbone, following the success of "Hound," was regarded as the quintessential Sherlock Holmes. He had the look, the accent, the demeanor that Sherlockians expected, and he would devote a major portion of his life interpreting the great detective in film, on radio, and on stage. In just the seven years between 1939 and 1946, he starred in fourteen films featuring Holmes. He also played the detective in a radio series called *The New Adventurers of Sherlock Holmes* that lasted for ten years. At the same time, Rathbone continued what he considered his more important work as a Shakespearean actor and as a serious stage performer. Like Conan Doyle, Rathbone became haunted by the Holmes persona and did his best to distance himself from the character, but it was to no avail. In all, he played Holmes in sixteen films and more than two hundred radio broadcasts. He claimed never to have been interviewed without being asked what it was like to be Sherlock Holmes. In public, on the streets and in restaurants, he was invariably greeted with, "Elementary, my dear Watson," "How's Dr. Watson?," or "Quick, Watson, the needle." Eventually, he came to accept the fact that he had become a dual personality and that there was no escape.

Rathbone continued to make films and stage appearances in other roles. He appeared in two Broadway musicals as Marley's ghost in *A Christmas Carol*, costarred in a number of movies with Vincent Price and Errol Flynn, recorded memorable readings of Edgar Allan Poe's works, and toured America and England in a one-man show entitled *In and Out of Character*. Rathbone died in 1967 at the age of seventy-five. He was knighted

The famous Rathbone profile

by King George VI for his theatrical achievements and made a member of "The Most Excellent Order of the British Empire" by Queen Elizabeth II. His 1939 film *The Hound of the Baskervilles* remains one of the most popular and beloved films of its era.

✻ ✻ ✻

Nigel Bruce played Dr. Watson in thirteen additional Sherlock Holmes movies, and his portrayals established the Watson character firmly in the public consciousness as a somewhat dim and bumbling companion to the detective—despite the fact that Watson is portrayed as capable and intelligent in the original Conan Doyle stories. Known as "Willie" to his friends, he became an important member of the British film colony in Hollywood and played important roles in a number of significant non-Holmes films, including *The Rains Came*, *Rebecca*, *Suspicion*, *The Corn Is Green*, and *Limelight*. In all, Bruce appeared in seventy-eight films over his career. He died of a heart attack in 1953 at age 58.

✻ ✻ ✻

Blitzen, the dog that played the title role in the movie, retired from film work after his one memorable performance in the title role in *The Hound of the Baskervilles*.

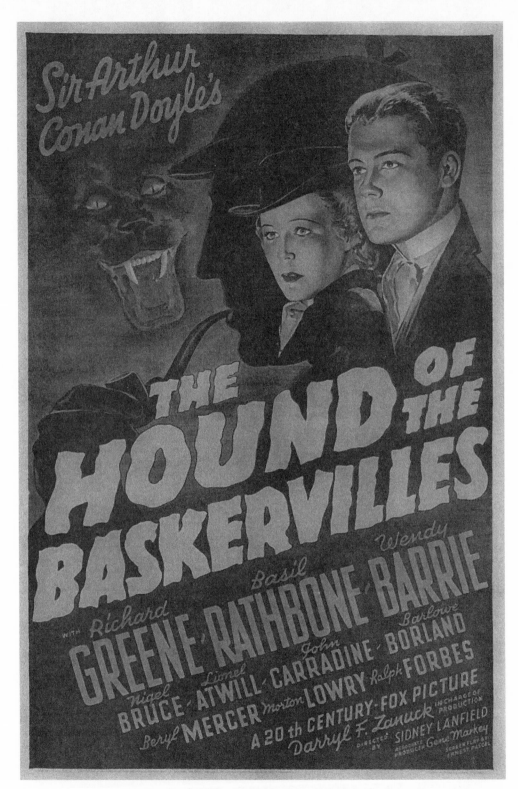

Poster for *The Hound of the Baskervilles*

THE HOUND OF THE BASKERVILLES
THE FINAL FACTS

Studio:	Twentieth Century Fox
Associate Producer:	Gene Markey
Director:	Sidney Lanfield
Screenplay:	Ernest Pascal
Original Story:	Sir Arthur Conan Doyle
Photographer:	Pervel Marley
Art Direction:	Richard Day and Hans Peters
Running Time:	82 minutes
Release Date:	March 31, 1939
Cost of Production:	$375,000 (est.)
Box Office (original run):	Unknown, but sufficient to inspire an additional thirteen Sherlock Holmes films starring Rathbone and Bruce

Cast

Sherlock Holmes.............. Basil Rathbone
Dr. Watson .... Nigel Bruce
Sir Henry Baskerville .... Richard Greene
John Stapleton .... Morton Lowry
Beryl Stapleton .... Wendy Barrie
Dr. Mortimer .... Lionel Atwill
Barryman.......................... John Carradine
Sir Hugo Baskerville......... Ralph Forbes
Mrs. Jennifer Mortimer.... Beryl Mercer
Sir Charles Baskerville..... Ian Maclaren
Mrs. Hudson .... Mary Gordon
The Convict .... Nigel DeBrulier
The Hound .... Chief (a.k.a. "Blitzen")

Awards

Nominated by the American Film Institute as one
of the Top Ten Mystery Films of All-Time.

The original novel

THE ADVENTURES OF HUCKLEBERRY FINN

THE STORY

It was a beautiful summer day as Samuel Clemens began the climb up through a sun-spattered glade to his gazebo at Quarry Farms. Thirty-seven wooden steps. Just enough of a climb to get his heart pumping—and just enough time to get his mind churning. Within minutes, it was in sight, and he had a sense of gratitude every time he saw it. Octagonal in shape, with a handsome peaked roof, it sat perched in isolated splendor above the rolling hills of upper New York, with spectacular views through windows on every side. Only a few years ago, it had been given to him as a surprise gift by his sister-in-law as a place where he could write in peace and solitude, and now it was his salvation.

He sensed that this was an important day. He was taking up a task that he had put aside more than once. He opened the

Clemens' writing gazebo

door and glanced around the room. There was his circular writing table, his straight-backed wicker chair, and two smaller chairs in case visitors came. This morning he had asked not to be disturbed. He sat down and studied the papers on his desk. He gathered together the pages of two stories that he had been working on, organized them a bit, then put them aside. Clemens then opened a drawer on his desk and took out a large pile of handwritten papers. There were more than four hundred of them and it required a little effort to lift them up. He placed them on the table in front of him and studied the top page for a moment. It read *Huckleberry Finn's Autobiography*. He had written that title almost seven years ago, but now it didn't seem quite right. He picked up his pen, crossed out those words, and above them wrote *Adventures of Huckleberry Finn (Tom Sawyer's Comrade)*. Then, because he now felt committed to this story, below his new title he carefully wrote "by Mark Twain." The time had come to tell the rest of the story.

He lit a cigar and reflected on the work he was now ready to do and how he had come to this place. Suddenly, old faces seemed to come out of the past. Old days began to troop by. Old voices greeted him. Old footsteps sounded in his ears.

✳ ✳ ✳

It had been a long road from Hannibal, Missouri. He had traveled that road for almost half a century and had enough experiences to fill a hundred books.

He had come into this world as Sam Clemens in 1835, heralded by that rare celestial spectacle called Halley's Comet. His early memories were all of Hannibal, and though Clemens would be a tireless traveler all his life, Hannibal would be with him wherever he went. He had spent his entire boyhood in Hannibal, a steamboat port on the Mississippi River, absorbing the character of its people, learning the rhythms and cadences of their language, and experiencing the beauty and the terrors of its great river.

Two Hannibal friends in particular would always haunt his memories. Tom Blankenship, the son of the town drunk, was the youngster he valued and admired most. Tom was mischievous, fun-loving, a bit of a troublemaker, always coming up with some scheme to keep his parents and elders on edge. The other was Anna Laura Hawkins, the pretty, blue-eyed girl that Sam first fell in love with and courted—but always from afar. Later on, Sam would change the names of both of these two Hannibal friends and make them world famous.

Samuel Clemens

When he was fourteen, Sam was apprenticed to his older brother as a typesetter—a skill he learned quickly and would value in some form or other the rest of his life. At the newspaper where he worked, he formed a love for words, read everything he could get his hands on, and eventually began to compose little articles and poems to make the publication more interesting. Interestingly, he was a little too shy and too playful to use his own name, so he would sign them "W. Epaminondas Adrastrus Blab." He liked the idea of having a *nom de plume*, and even in his early writings his biting and whimsical sense of humor was on display.

At seventeen, he left Hannibal to make his fortune in the larger world. Armed with his typesetting skills, he worked in St. Louis, Philadelphia, Cincinnati, and New York. He continued to write articles and stories, sending them to various publications, now signing them "Thomas Jefferson Snodgrass." And he kept on the move.

He would be a wanderer all his life, always seeking new places, new faces, new experiences. Yet he never forgot the joys and mysteries of the Mississippi River and so, when he tired of the printing trade, he went back to the river. In New Orleans, he signed on as an apprentice riverboat pilot under the tutelage of the famed Captain Horace Bixby. Over the next several years, he would learn all 1,200 miles of the Mississippi River, and he became an ardent student of its currents, its dangers, and its idiosyncrasies. And at all times, he studied the people of the river and the river towns—how they looked, how they talked, what they wore, what they thought.

When the Civil War erupted in 1861, Twain left the river and served briefly in a local militia and then, when the militia disbanded, he took off with his brother for Nevada, where he was sure he could find riches working in the mountains as a silver miner. When he failed at silver mining, he resettled in Virginia City, a rough and tough boomtown in Nevada, situated at the foothills of the Sierra Nevadas. There he wrote a humorous account of his westerly travels for a newspaper, and he signed the article with still another manufactured name. This time he was "Mark Twain."

SAM CLEMENS ON THE MOVE

After a stint as a reporter and journalist for the Virginia City *Territorial Enterprise*, Clemens moved on to San Francisco, where he met such well-known writers of the time as Bret Harte and Artemus Ward. But their influences did not bring him writing success. At one point, lonely and without funds, he contemplated suicide. Then, quite suddenly, his fortunes turned. After hearing a miner tell a humorous story about a gambling experience, Clemens revised the tale, embellished it, wrote it in the dialect of the time, and sent it to a New York weekly, the *Saturday Express*. The story, called "The Celebrated Jumping Frog of Calaveras County," became an instant hit with readers throughout the East and brought him sudden fame. Clemens—and Mark Twain—was on his way as a writer.

When a Sacramento newspaper offered him the chance to sail to Hawaii, Clemens jumped at the opportunity. His accounts of that trip brought him further attention and, on his return, he discovered he could

Mark Twain

Mark Twain at his writing desk

make money lecturing on his experiences in the Hawaiian islands, which were then called the Sandwich Islands. From that point on, he had two useful and money-making skills—writing and lecturing. He would make the most of them for the rest of his life.

In 1867, Clemens traveled through Europe and the Middle East, chronicling his experiences in a successful book called *The Innocents Abroad*. By this time, Sam had acquired almost a dual personality—Samuel Clemens, the family man (he married in 1869 and fathered three daughters), and Mark Twain, the respected and admired, as well as hilarious and insightful, author.

For the next fifteen years, Twain continued to propel his successful writing career and to tell his stories to adoring audiences. In 1876, his fame and celebrity took another major leap forward with the publication of *The Adventures of Tom Sawyer*.

The World Meets Tom Sawyer

For two years during the mid-1870s, Clemens worked on and off on the story of Tom Sawyer. When he finally completed it, he sent it first to his publisher in England, a technique the author had used before to protect his copyright there. But within just a few months, a pirated edition appeared in Canada, and the book became so popular that copies were brought into the United States and were widely read long before its publication in New York. Clemens would always claim it cost him valuable sales and commissions. The book was sold only by subscription. Book agents nationwide then delivered the book personally once it was available. Only later would it be sold in retail establishments. Nevertheless, with all these birth pangs, fifteen thousand copies of *The Adventures of Tom Sawyer* were sold in its opening weeks and twenty-seven thousand in its first year. Still, it would take another Twain book, published nine years later, to turn *The Adventures of Tom Sawyer* into a global phenomenon.

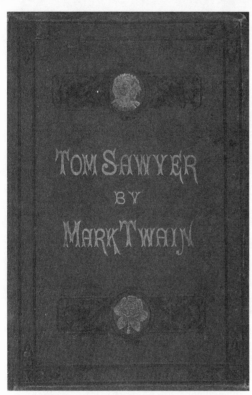

The first edition of *Tom Sawyer*

In *The Adventures of Tom Sawyer*, Twain created a mythic version of American boyhood, calling up memories and emotions that delighted both its young and older readers. Tom and his raffish friend, Huckleberry Finn, had experiences and adventures that planted themselves firmly in the American psyche. Tom lived in the fictional Mississippi river town of St. Petersburg (think Hannibal) with his Aunt Polly. He played hooky from school, got into fights, persuaded friends of the joys of whitewashing his aunt's fence, failed to remember his Bible verses, fell in love with the pretty Becky Thatcher, tried to cure warts by visiting a cemetery in the dead of night, witnessed a murder, took "blood oaths," ran away, attended his own funeral, hunted for treasure, dealt with threats and dangers presented by the murderous "Injun Joe," got lost in a cave, found a treasure box with his friend Huck and got rich, and talked Huck into being adopted by the Widow Douglas, despite the terrible prospect that she would "civilize" him.

The principal characters in the novel were based, in good part, on acquaintances of his youth in Hannibal. Becky Thatcher was born out of his memory of Laura Hawkins, the pretty lass he knew during his boyhood. Huckleberry Finn was dredged up out of his memories of the irascible Tom Blankenship, the friend he admired most as he was growing up. Tom himself was based largely on the youngster that Twain remembered best—Sam Clemens.

THE BIRTH OF HUCKLEBERRY FINN

As fond as readers were of the lovable Tom Sawyer, it was the puckish Huck Finn who stayed in many of their minds—including the author's. There was more gold to be mined out of Finn, and it was not too long after the publication of *The Adventures of Tom Sawyer* that Twain wrote one day on a clear piece of writing paper the words *Huckleberry Finn's Autobiography*. If a story about Finn were to be told, it would be told in his Huck's own words.

Mark Twain was now at the peak of his powers—and Samuel Clemens turned him loose. An almost constant stream of literature of all kinds poured forth from his pen—letters, monographs, essays, political columns, and short stories. And Twain's books and stories kept coming: *A Tramp Abroad*, *The Stolen White Elephant*, *Punch Brothers and Other Stories*, and *The Prince and the Pauper*. He was now the richest, best-known, and most prolific writer in America. And, somewhere over this period, he began the first-person narrative about Huckleberry Finn.

Twain was not above capitalizing on the popularity of Tom Sawyer, and so he began, "You will not know about me without you have read a book by the name of *The Adventures of Tom Sawyer*, but that ain't no matter. That book was made by Mr. Mark Twain, and he told the truth, mainly." This first sentence got Twain's novel off to a rollicking start, and it set the tone for all the words that came after. Twain was writing in the first person and in the everyday vernacular of mid-century Hannibal. He wrote swiftly and steadily, pausing only to relight his pipe or to search for a right word. Each word was important, for as Twain had earlier written, "The difference between the right word and the almost right word is the difference between lightning and a lightning bug."

And so, during the late months of 1883, Twain, writing at warp speed, propelled Huck's tale forward—completing 446 pages of written text in a matter of weeks. Every evening he would leave his writing cottage and return to the house with the day's manuscript under his arm. Then he would gather his family and whatever guests happened to be visiting, and he would read to them what he had written that day. As he read, he studied their reactions and their attentiveness. He could tell they loved what they were hearing. There was no doubt that they were listening to a remarkable story. They learned that Huck Finn and his old pal Tom Sawyer were right where they had been left at the end of Tom's book—with both of them suffering under the efforts of their betters to "civilize" them.

TWAIN STARTS THE STORY

(Huck is now subject to the guardianship and strictures of Widow Douglas. Tom helps Huck escape from the house at night and they sneak past the widow's slave, Jim. Huck's freedom is short lived as he is quickly captured by his shiftless, hard-drinking "Pap," who wants the gold treasure he believes the boys have found. He locks Huck in his cabin by the river, but Huck again escapes, this time leaving a trail of pig blood to the river in an effort to fake his death. Huck sets off down the river in a boat and winds up on an island where he encounters Jim, who is now a runaway slave. Jim is trying to get to Cairo, Illinois, where he can be a free man. The two slowly become fast friends

as they exchange views on life, slavery, and "all manner of things." They find a raft which they decide to use to travel the river to Cairo, but in the night and the fog, they drift right past their destination and find themselves in a place where Jim is sure to be captured.)

And then, for some reason, Twain stopped writing the novel. Perhaps he was uncertain where the plot should go next—or he was bored with the story—or he had to take up other projects. He left Huckleberry Finn stuck right where he was—right in the middle of the Mississippi River. It wasn't until several months later that he picked up the narrative and rescued Huck and Jim.

(Drifting on the flooded river, they come on an old house floating by. In the house Jim finds a dead body, but he will not let Huck look at the man's face. To find out what is happening

HUCK AND HIS FATHER.

Huck and Pap (original
drawing from the novel)

in the area, Huck dresses as a girl, but he is quickly unmasked. He returns to tell Jim that there is a manhunt out for him. Together they drift on in the raft until they are swamped by a steamship. Huck and Jim separate and Huck is given shelter by a prosperous family named Grangerford. This involves him in a deadly blood feud with another family.)

Once again, Twain put his pen down and stopped writing about Huckleberry Finn. This time, he would give him a long rest. He went on to other projects. He was working on two other novels—*The Prince and the Pauper* and *A Connecticut Yankee in King Arthur's Court*. At one point, he suggested to his publisher that several of these books might be published together in a single volume. The publisher, fortunately for

THE WRECK.

Original drawing from the novel

posterity, thought this was a bad idea. *The Prince and the Pauper* was published on its own in 1879.

Twain's 662 handwritten manuscript pages of *The Adventures of Huckleberry Finn* rested in the dark of his desk drawer for almost five years. Twain wrote his publisher, saying, "I like it only tolerably well, and may possibly pigeonhole or burn it when it is done."

During that time away from telling Huck's story, Clemens embarked on an extraordinary odyssey—he traveled the length of the Mississippi River on a riverboat from St. Louis to New Orleans and then back up to Minneapolis. He spent almost two months on the river and traveled more than two thousand miles—drinking in the sights and sounds of his youth, watching, studying, listening, and reflecting. He returned to his work refreshed in spirit and drenched in the recollections of his earlier days on the river.

Once Again, Twain Picks Up the Story

Now, back in his writing gazebo in Elmira, Twain had pulled Huckleberry Finn's story out into the light once again, placed the pages back on his desk, changed the title from *Huckleberry Finn's Autobiography* to *The Adventures of Huckleberry Finn (Tom Sawyer's Comrade)*, and, after reflecting on where he had been with this story and where he would take it, he took up his pen and began writing almost without pause. When his arthritic right hand wearied, he would switch the pen to his left hand and continue writing. He would later tell a friend that he had become "fully invested" in the book and was writing up to four thousand words a day.

(Huck has survived the feud, narrowly avoiding his own death, and reuniting with Jim on the raft. They float farther down the river and encounter two con men, one who claims to be the son of an English duke, the other the rightful King of France. The two grifters involve Huck in a series of confidence schemes, including a three-night theatrical engagement in which they pretend to be famous English actors.

Twain relaxing on a riverboat

Jim and Huck resume their journey down the river with the Duke and the King until they reach the next river town. The two con men then attempt to impersonate the heirs of a recently deceased man named "Wilkes." They succeed in fooling the townspeople and wind up with Wilkes' inheritance. Huck tries to steal the money back from the two fake royals as they sleep. In danger of discovery, he hides the money in Wilkes' coffin, and the money is subsequently buried with the deceased. Eventually, Jim is recaptured and held prisoner on the farm of Silas and Sally Phelps, Tom Sawyer's aunt and uncle. Huck, alone in the hut on the raft, debates with

Huck and Jim guide the raft (original drawing from the novel)

himself as to whether or not he should write a letter to Miss Watson telling her where her escaped slave is. He writes the letter, but then in an act of pure humanity, he destroys it, even though he thinks his decision is contrary to God's law and that his action may condemn him to hell.

Huck then runs into Tom, who is visiting the Phelpses, and Tom tells Huck everything that has happened and the two conspire to free Jim. Jim, in the meantime, has told the local townspeople who the fake Duke and King are, and when they show up in town, they are tarred and feathered. Instead of just releasing Jim from the shed in which he is being held, Huck and Jim contrive elaborate schemes and charades. Jim escapes. Tom is shot in the leg and Jim remains with him even though he knows it will mean certain recapture. The doctor treating Tom betrays Jim to a passing boat, and he is captured and returned to the Phelps family. Huck later learns that Jim has been freed because of the death of his owner. Jim tells Huck that the dead man they found on the floating house was actually Huck's father. Rather than return to St. Petersburg, Huck announces he is going to flee west to Indian territory.)

Twain put his finishing touches on his novel in September of 1883 and, rather than sending it directly to the publisher, he decided to have the entire manuscript typed on a newfangled invention called a "typewriter." Twain hired a pair of lady typists to employ their new skills to the hundreds of handwritten pages he had just completed. Thus, *The Adventures of Huckleberry Finn* became the first novel ever sent to an American publisher in typed form.

Twain's books required illustrations, as readers wanted to see the action depicted in his stories and because Twain himself felt they were important for continuity and to help sales. Edwin Windsor Kemble, a young California illustrator, was selected for the task. In all, Kemble produced 175 drawings before Twain would approve the sketches that would appear in the book.

The Adventures of Huckleberry Finn was finally published in December of 1884. Twain again saw to it that his book was first published in England to assure his copyright there, and, once again, it appeared first in Canada in pirated editions before being published in America. This infuriated Twain because he was sure the Canadian version stole sales from his U.S. sales. He needn't have worried. Before spring of 1885, more than twenty-five thousand copies had been sold and, just ten days later, the number jumped to thirty-nine thousand. *The Adventures of Huckleberry Finn* was an international hit.

THE BEWILDERED CRITICS

Literary critics seemed not to know what to think about *The Adventures of Huckleberry Finn*. The *New York World* was offended by the book's "humor of a very low order, wit and literary ability wasted on a pitiable exhibition of irreverence and vulgarity"…but then conceded that "a few good things are dropped amid a mass of rubbish." The *Boston Bulletin* railed against the book's "coarseness and bad taste." The book's use of vernacular language and grammar—and the sympathetic treatment of the slave Jim—seemed to put these critics off their game. Several libraries banned the book altogether, with one citing the book as "more suited to the slums than to intelligent, respectable people."

THE ERECTION EDITION

As *The Adventures of Huckleberry Finn* was rolling off the presses, an alert pressman studied Kemble's drawings to see how they were reproducing, and he made an astonishing discovery. Someone— possibly Kemble in a naughty mood or, more likely, an engraver with a sense of humor—had added a few strokes to the illustration of Uncle Silas as he thrust out his pelvic area toward Huck in a gesture of confrontation. The added strokes made it distressingly clear that Uncle Silas had an erection.

UNCLE SILAS IN DANGER.

The altered drawing

The minute the publisher was alerted, he ordered the presses to be stopped. Fortunately, only 250 copies of the altered book had been printed and salesmen were ordered to return any that were already in circulation. When Twain heard about the mishap, he thought it was hilarious.

As time went on, *The Adventures of Huckleberry Finn* grew both in popularity and in critical acclaim. Over the next century, it came to be almost required childhood reading, and it is not an exaggeration to say that it is one of America's most beloved books.

Pulitzer Prize winner Ron Powers has called *The Adventures of Huckleberry Finn* a "consensus masterpiece." Writer Ernest Hemingway declared it to be "the great American novel," stating that "all American literature comes from this book." Over the years, the book has sold millions of copies and has been translated into more than fifty different languages. It has become, truly, a story for all the ages.

Huck Goes to the Movies

The first film adaptation of *The Adventures of Huckleberry Finn* was made in 1920, thirty-six years after the publication of the novel. The film industry was still in its infancy and sound had not yet come to the screen. Famous Players-Lasky Corporation had turned two earlier Twain stories into movies, *Tom Sawyer* and *Huck and Tom*. Both had been successful, so it was logical that *The Adventures of Huckleberry Finn* should follow. It was a faithful adaptation of the story and it was filmed primarily on-site in Hannibal, Missouri. As a result, the film has a certain authenticity that later films would lack. The *New York Times* said, "No matter what its shortcomings may be, it should be a joy to everyone." More important, it did what Hollywood films are supposed to do: It made money.

When sound came to motion pictures in the later 1920s, it was inevitable that another *The Adventures of Huckleberry Finn* would have to be made. In 1931 Paramount Pictures took up the task. Paramount took significant liberties with Twain's novel. The relationship between Huck and Jim is downplayed and there is a much enhanced and complicated plot involving Huck, Tom Sawyer, and Becky Thatcher. A minimum amount of time is spent on the raft cruising the Mississippi and the maturing of Huck's attitude toward Jim virtually disappears. At the end, Huck and Becky kiss. Nevertheless, the acting is for the most part excellent and many of the iconic scenes from the novel were preserved. Like the first "Huck" movie, this one did its job: It also made money.

Two years later, in 1933, MGM paid Paramount $30,000 for the movie rights to *The Adventures of Huckleberry Finn*. It is not clear what MGM was buying—or why it paid so much. Copyright law at the time of the publication of Twain's novel protected such a work for fourteen years, with an option to renew the copyright for another fourteen. This would mean that Twain's copyright expired in 1899 at the latest. There is no evidence that either Famous Players-Lasky or Paramount Pictures paid any money to the Twain estate, nor would it seem logical that they would be required to. So, it is unclear why

Child actors from the early adaptation of Huckleberry Finn

MGM could not have simply taken the novel, which was now clearly in the public domain, and adapted it for its own film. It also seems like an extraordinary amount of money to have been paid for any film rights at that time. Four years later, David O. Selznick would pay an identical amount of money for the film rights to *Gone with the Wind*.

At any rate, MGM, having purchased the rights to make its own version of *The Adventures of Huckleberry Finn*, then seemed in no hurry to capitalize on the investment. On October 19, 1936, Luella Parsons reported in her influential column that "David O. Selznick is temporarily shelving *The Adventures of Huckleberry Finn* because he can't find the right boy for the role." Selznick couldn't have been looking very hard, because "the boy" was already under contract to MGM.

"The Mick"

He came into this world as Joe Yule Jr., and, while he was not literally born on the stage, it was a near thing. His parents were both vaudeville performers: Joe Sr. was a comedian and his mother was a chorus dancer. Before Joe Jr. was eighteen months old, he was part of their act—playing harmonica and making faces at the audience. By the time he was five years old, he was a stage veteran.

Realizing her youngster had genuine talent, Joe's mother packed their suitcases and headed for Hollywood where hundreds of other stage mothers were already in residence, trying to get their moppets into movies. The competition was fierce, but Joe Jr. had an advantage: He was short. At casting calls for children's roles, he would pretend to be several years younger than he actually was and his added maturity over the other contenders frequently got him the job. He also made stage appearances in local theaters, singing, dancing, and reciting, while always augmenting the impact of his performance by pretending to be younger than he was. In his minor film roles, he frequently played midgets—or tough, wiseacre kids. He got good reviews from the beginning, directors started to take notice, and he signed on with an experienced agent.

RKO was casting for a continuing lead role in a series of short films based on a cartoon script called "Toonville Trolley." The main character was a self-assured, swaggering, tough kid named Mickey McGuire, who was always creating trouble. Fifty child actors auditioned, all of them about the same size as Joe Jr.—but, of course, younger. Joe got the job, signed a contract for five dollars a day, and changed his name to "Mickey McGuire."

As Mickey, he starred in more than sixty short, two-reel films over a four-year period. Most of them were shot in less than a week and the work was grueling. The Mickey McGuire comedies were a huge success at the box office, and Joe became so identified with the role that his mother had his name legally changed to Mickey McGuire to fit his screen persona. For a while, "Mickey McGuire" became a popular synonym for a brash, wiseacre, smart-alecky kid. It is said that Walt Disney named his mouse after the child star.

When the series ended— after twenty-one silent films and more than forty talkies— Mickey went briefly back to vaudeville, where he could cash in on his newfound celebrity. He still did an occasional

Earliest photo taken
of Mickey Rooney

picture, usually performing minor roles. One day, when he was about to sign for a minor part in a Universal picture called *The Information Kid*, the studio told him they did not want him identified with his Mickey McGuire series. At first, they suggested he go back to "Joe Yule Jr.," but Mickey was reluctant. They considered "Mickey Yule," but Mick didn't like that either. Everyone finally agreed on "Mickey Rooney." Later, the name was cleared with the legal department and Mickey was told when he reported for work, "Well, kid, that's your new name—Mickey Rooney."

In 1932, at the age of twelve, Mickey had his first starring role in a major film using his new name. He costarred with Tom Mix in a film called *My Pal, the King*. Rooney played the part of a seven-year-old kid who was saved by Tom Mix from an evildoer. Universal paid him $250—and the *New York Times* spelled his name right and gave him a good review. The next year he made six movies for Universal.

Rooney as Mickey McGuire

MICKEY GROWS UP

Rooney was now thirteen and was a superb and enthusiastic athlete. He played running back on a football team of Hollywood youngsters and he took up both tennis and table tennis, winning the Junior Table Tennis Championship of Southern California.

Rooney's movie career began to stagnate at Universal and his contract was running out. He began to spend more and more time on athletics. While competing in a table tennis tournament at the Ambassador Hotel, Rooney started mugging for the audience, making wisecracks, and generally turning the tournament into a "Mickey Rooney Show." As it happened, David O. Selznick, the son-in-law of MGM head Louis B. Mayer and an independent producer within the studio, was in the audience. The next day, Selznick went to Mayer and said, "We got to sign a kid I saw perform yesterday. He is just sensational. His name is

Mickey Rooney. He used to be Mickey McGuire." Mayer was quick with his reply: "Oh, him. David, he's a has-been!" But Selznick was persistent; he eventually wore Mayer down, and MGM put Rooney under contract. This was a career-changing event for Mickey. MGM was Hollywood's biggest studio, with twenty-two sound stages spread over a 180-acre lot, four thousand employees, its own police and fire departments, and even its own operating oil well. Some of Hollywood's most glittering stars were under contract to the studio, including Wallace Beery, Clark Gable, William Powell, Joan Crawford, Greta Garbo, and Jean Harlow. Now, Mickey Rooney was one of them.

Rooney was put to work right away, performing in four pictures the first year. Then MGM loaned Rooney out to other studios for a high price—four pictures at Universal, then another at Warner Brothers, and still another at Columbia. Rooney was becoming a star in his own right and MGM was cashing in. As for Rooney, he was making $150 a week.

Even though he was not getting rich, Rooney was establishing a reputation as a dependable performer with box office appeal. Over the next several years, he starred or costarred in dozens of films. This was the era of mass movie production at MGM, with films being cranked out at an average of one a week and production schedules limited to a matter of a few months, sometimes even a few weeks.

Then, in 1937, a story editor named Sam Marx talked MGM into paying $5,000 for a play called "Skidding." Marx rewrote it for film, changed the name to *A Family Affair*, and talked Mayer out of a production budget of $185,000. Lionel Barrymore and Spring Byington were cast as the parents of a rascally, but basically nice, young son. That role went to Mickey Rooney. The young son in the film was named Andy Hardy.

✳ ✳ ✳

Not much was expected of the film, but audiences loved it—and they loved Andy Hardy. The film made more than half a million dollars for MGM. One theater owner wired the studio: "For God's sake, let's have more of that Rooney kid. The kid's a goldmine!" MGM got the message and, over the next two years, Rooney starred in seventeen more "Andy Hardy" films.

In a way, Mickey Rooney became Andy Hardy. In the public consciousness, Andy was the teenager any mother could love, and he lived in an idealized white-fenced house with an idealized American family. The Hardys portrayed a family that every theatergoing family wanted to be like and Andy was the son they wished they had. Even

Rooney the megastar

more important for MGM, the Andy Hardy films were flooding money into the coffers. Andy Hardy was the studio's most prized possession. And that's why Mickey Rooney—not Andy Hardy—was giving MGM a headache.

Mickey, at age nineteen, had become a well-known Hollywood lothario; he was pictured constantly on the arms of willing starlets, making himself juicy fodder for the industry's gossip columns. MGM began to worry that Mickey might be sullying the image of their moneymaking Andy Hardy. Finally, none other than studio head Louis B. Mayer summoned Rooney into his palatial office. Mayer tried being subtle: "Mickey, I hear you've never met a pretty girl you didn't like." Mickey played dumb, making some offhand remark about kissing the occasional girl. Mayer decided subtlety wasn't going to work: "Look, Mickey, I'm not talking about kissing. I'm talking about fucking!" Rooney got the message and promised, not necessarily to reform, but to do his best to stay out of the newspapers.

By 1938, Mickey Rooney was the biggest box office star in Hollywood, but he was concerned about being typecast as Andy Hardy.

So it was with some sense of relief that, in the summer of that year, he was told that he was to star in a major MGM picture, *The Adventures of Huckleberry Finn*. Rooney was delighted with both the role and the script, and he started right away working with MGM's diction coach to perfect his mid-century, small-town Missouri accent.

THE "HUCK" TEAM FILLS OUT

Casting of the part of the slave Jim would be key to the film's success. There were a number of excellent black actors working in Hollywood in the 1930s, but they tended to play minor characters or, more frequently, servants. A number of actors auditioned for the part—and the clear winner to play the runaway slave was Rex Ingram.

Ingram was an experienced stage and film actor who had performed in a number of silent films, including several Tarzan movies. But he flowered when talkies came in because of his strong, resonant voice. He had a featured role in the 1936 film *Green Pastures*. Ingram brought everything that was needed to the role of Jim—a handsome face, a sympathetic nature, sound acting talent, and obvious intelligence. (He was the first African American to ever win a Phi Beta Kappa key from Northwestern University.)

The rest of the roles were quickly filled. The key supporting roles of "The King" and "The Duke" went to two veteran character actors, Walter Connolly and William Frawley. Connolly was a longtime Broadway performer with twenty-two films on his résumé. He had also played Claudette Colbert's father in *It Happened One Night*, the hit film of the year before, and he had a key role with Paul Muni in *The Good Earth*. Frawley, a longtime contract player with Paramount, was loaned out to MGM for his role in *The Adventures of Huckleberry Finn*.

MGM had a full stable of talented directors. One of them, Richard Thorpe, was a veteran of such hits as *Notorious but Nice*, *Green Eyes*, and *The Crowd Roars*. However, he didn't appear to be available for "Huck" because he was hard at work on another MGM production, *The Wizard of Oz*. But the powers at MGM decided early on that Thorpe's hard work on "Wizard" wasn't getting the job done. He was fired off the film and

Joe Mankiewicz, the studio producer on *The Adventures of Huckleberry Finn*, grabbed Thorpe for his own film.

Thorpe was a good choice. He was competent without being brilliant, and workmanlike instead of inspired. He had a reputation for "getting the job done," frequently settling for a single take on scenes. This was fine with Mickey, who was himself displeased with directors who insisted on shooting multiple takes in order to protect themselves.

Fortunately for the film, Thorpe brought two major contributors with him when he moved over from *The Wizard of Oz* to "Huck": art director Cedric Gibbons and set designer Edwin Willis. Though both continued to work on "Oz" at the same time, they made significant contributions to the success of *The Adventures of Huckleberry Finn*.

WRITING "HUCK" DOWN TO SIZE

Screenwriter Hugo Butler was given the task of translating Twain's sprawling novel into an hour and half of movie film. Butler was a

Rex Ingram

highly regarded journalist and an experienced playwright who had only recently come to Hollywood and to MGM. *The Adventures of Huckleberry Finn* was his first major film assignment.

He believed in David O. Selznick's dictum that the way to harness a long story that was well known by the public was to preserve the major scenes and to retain the lines the audiences would be likely to remember. Butler did a creditable job and achieved a workable script that was faithful to the main parts of the Twain story.

But Butler also did something else: He added some strong social content that Twain never intended. His inclusion of pointed antidiscrimination language, while certainly not extreme by today's standards, caused some criticism. Rooney himself later recalled that "a few critics wondered why the screenwriter had to turn Huck Finn into a premature member of the civil rights movement, and so did the public."

Of course, no movie script of the hour-and-a-half length demanded by movie theater operators could fully contain the magic of Twain's work, but Butler gave it a good try.

The Script for
The Adventures of Huckleberry Finn

Huck is seen absent from school. He is fishing at the river when his gang shows up and Huck realizes he will not be promoted at school. At home with the Widow Douglas and the kindly Miss Watson, he is served dinner by the widow's slave, Jim. He learns that Jim's wife and children are already in a free state. Huck goes to his room and finds his drunken "Pap" is there. "Pap" tell the ladies he will sell Huck to them for $800. Huck flees the house and is then kidnapped by "Pap" and locked up in a cabin by the river. He escapes and leaves evidence that he has been murdered. He takes a boat to an island where he finds Jim, who has also escaped. Huck poses as a girl and returns to town, where he discovers that Jim is suspected of his murder. Huck and Jim return to the raft and drift to an island where Jim discovers Huck's dead father in a flood-floated house. As they raft farther down the river, Huck and Jim become friends, talking about life and freedom. Jim's goal is to make it to Cairo, where he will be free.

The two drifters are threatened by a charging steamboat from which they see two men thrown into the water. They rescue the two men. One claims to be the Duke of Bridgewater, the other the King of France. The two con men devise a plan to raise money and put on a theatrical showing of "Romeo and Juliet" in a port town. They raise enough money to arrive in style at another town, claiming to be the rightful heirs to the estate of a recently deceased gentleman of means. They manage to steal $2,000 in gold from the family, money which Huck, in turn, steals from them. Huck loses the gold when, afraid of being caught, he hides the money in a casket. Huck is then befriended by a trustee of the estate who is also a riverboat captain.

Huck reunites with Jim, telling him that the steamboat captain is going to take them to Cairo. Jim tells Huck that the dead man in the house was his "Pap." Huck feels betrayed and, in fleeing from Jim, he is bitten by a rattlesnake. To prove his friendship, Jim carries Huck into town to find a doctor. Jim is then captured and sent back to be tried for Huck's murder. As Huck recovers, Jim is placed on trial and convicted. Huck realizes he must reappear to prove Jim's innocence. There is a race against time as Huck hurries home on his benefactor's steamboat and Jim is threatened by vigilantes. Huck arrives just in time to save Jim. Back at the Widow Douglas' home, Huck convinces her to free Jim.

Huck fakes his own death.

Huck promises to reform and Jim is freed to rejoin his family in Cairo. In the final scene, Huck is once again caught stoking on his pipe and, barefooted, he walks away from the camera.

THE END

There are a number of significant differences between the movie plot and the Twain novel. Perhaps the most important is the absence of Tom Sawyer. In the novel, Tom plays a significant role in the story as Huck's companion-in-mischief, both at the beginning of the tale and at the conclusion. His absence is probably best explained by the conviction of Louis B. Mayer, the head of MGM, that it is the stars who make the movie and attract the audience. Rooney was a true megastar at MGM and the presence of another mischievous lad in the film would only detract from Rooney's performance and complicate the film. Also, the plot had to be simplified in order to keep the film within the ninety minutes that theater owners found acceptable. Tom Sawyer was expendable.

Another important change is in the conclusion of the story. In the novel, Huck and Tom construct elaborate plans to free the captive Jim who is kept prisoner at the Phelps property. In the movie, Jim is imprisoned and Huck races to see that he is freed. In effect, the last three chapters of Twain's work were chopped out.

Also missing is the entire episode in which Huck is sheltered by the Grangerford family, during which the feud with another family puts Huck in danger of his own life. This excision is certainly understandable as it takes time to develop the story line and would certainly slow down the film and interrupt the flow of the developing relationship between Huck and Jim.

Dr. Robinson, who exposes the con men in the book, becomes Captain Brady, a riverboat captain, in the movie. This is a matter of convenience because it enables the dramatic riverboat race in order to save Jim to take place.

A quotation on the evil of slavery by Abraham Lincoln is recited by Captain Brady, gratuitously inserted to point up the moral of the story. And an incident in the novel in which Jim is bitten by a rattlesnake is changed to make Huck the victim. This change is what motivates Jim to save Huck and risk his own freedom and leads to the new ending of the story.

Unhappily, one of the most memorable and heralded lines in the novel was omitted. In Twain's story, Huck ponders what to do about helping Jim to freedom and he writes a letter telling Jim's owner where Jim is. He then contemplates the letter, debating whether to send it or destroy it. He recites his belief that not sending it would be a serious crime and could condemn him to hell. Finally, he tears up the letter and declares, "Well, then, I'll go to hell!" Many critics claim this to be one of the greatest single lines in American literature—a turning point not just in Huck's life but also a statement of America's revised attitude toward slavery. Perhaps its absence is compensated somewhat by a line given to Huck in the film in which he pleads for Jim's freedom: "It's just not right for one human being to own another human being." But, all in all, it seems like a somewhat preachy and inadequate substitute.

One other thing is missing in the movie: the word "nigger." This word appears 219 times in Twain's novel. It was part of Twain's search for authentic Southern language and dialect. Use of the word was controversial from the outset, and the book was branded as racist in many quarters. The controversy continues to this day. *The Adventures of Huckleberry Finn* has become one of the most banned books in American library history. The book has also been published with the word "nigger" changed to "negro" or "slave." Almost all modern scholars, however, argue that, despite Twain's profligate use of the word "nigger," the story is essentially antiracist and the portrayal of Jim is sympathetic throughout the novel. In the film, the word "negro" is used twice and Jim is once ungraciously referred to as "that sort."

Despite all the liberties taken with Twain's work, Hugo Butler had managed to preserve the essence of the novel in his script. The relationship between Huck and Jim remained. The moral core of the script and most of the principal scenes that moviegoers would expect to see would be there on the screen. Butler's script was approved by MGM with few changes, and the film was hurried into production.

MICKEY BECOMES HUCK

Filming for *The Adventures of Huckleberry Finn* got under way on November 19, 1938, and shooting would continue until January of 1939. The shooting was for the most part uneventful, occurring on what was called a "happy set." Mickey and Rex got along extremely well. Both were professionals, fast studies, and anxious to do well on the first take. In one of the early scenes at the Widow Douglas' house, Thorpe called Mickey back for a redo. Rooney protested mildly, "Hey, I thought it was pretty good!" Replied Thorpe, "Sorry, Mickey, we had a shadow from the boom mike." Rooney understood and did the scene over again without complaint.

All of the early scenes at the widow's house were shot on a constructed stage set at MGM and the closing scenes were shot at the same time. The filming was quickly moved to Northern California and the Sacramento River, where the river scenes were shot. The citizens of the towns of Hood, Ryde, Stockton, and Walnut Grove, all near the lower reaches of the river, were enthralled at the sight of movie cameras and, more important, of movie stars in their midst. Mickey himself was hailed as a celebrity wherever he went. The locals were also surprised to see that wherever Mickey went, he was accompanied by someone who looked very much like him.

MICKEY DOUBLES UP

The "double" was a new friend of Mickey's named Dick Paxton. Just one month earlier, Mickey had been roller-skating at an arena in Encino when he noticed a young man who looked familiar. He looked familiar because he resembled the image that Mickey saw every day in the mirror. Intrigued, he introduced himself, noticing at the same time this stranger was also about his height. The two of them hit it

Jim and Huck with the King and the Duke

The unsuccessful attempt at *Romeo and Juliet*

off right away and, after an hour or so of conversation, Mickey asked
Dick if he was interested in working in films. When Dick said yes,
Mickey replied, "How would you like to be my double? I'm starting
a new film this week about Huckleberry Finn and I need a stand-in."
"What's a stand-in?" asked Dick. Mickey replied, "You learn my part.
Then you help the camera get ready for each scene by walking through
my moves." Dick asked why Mickey didn't do that himself. Mickey
answered that at MGM every star had to have a double. He was a star
so they expected him to have a double. It was that simple.

Paxton seemed to catch on to the job right away, reading the
script quickly, even putting the crew through its paces before they
were ready for Mickey to do the scene. Director Thorpe was pleased
with Mickey's "discovery" and put him to good use. Their work on the
river included a scene in which Huck dives into the water to retrieve a
drifting boat. Thorpe suggested that Paxton do the scene because the
water was freezing cold. "Mickey," he said, "you could catch pneumonia
and that would play hell with the shooting schedule. It's a long shot and
no one will know the difference." So Paxton dove in and did the scene.
Then Mickey decided he could do it better, so he dove in and did the
scene again. Then Dick did it again just for the fun of it. There is no way
of knowing which actor's take actually appears in the final film.

Mickey Rooney wasn't the only celebrity working in the area.
Max Baer, the one-time heavyweight champion of the world, was there
training for his upcoming fight with boxer Lou Nova. Baer was an
actor himself and had appeared in a number of films, including *The
Prizefighter and the Lady,* in which he played opposite Myrna Loy and
Walter Huston. Max and Mickey developed a quick friendship and
would frequently jog together along the riverbank road before the day's
filming began.

There were a number of advantages in filming the river scenes
on the Sacramento River. The first, of course, was proximity. It was
relatively easy for the actors and film crew to transport their equipment
and their operation to Northern California instead of traveling to
Missouri. Equally important was the fact that there was a fully
operating and authentic steamboat available on the Sacramento River.

Ingram studying the script

The *Delta Queen* looked for all the world like a Mississippi riverboat from the nineteenth century. Built just a decade earlier in 1927, the "Queen" was propelled by an immense rear paddlewheel and was outfitted with lavish and authentic decorations. Stretching 285 feet in length, the "Queen" made an imposing presence on the river—and in the film. The ship makes more than a dozen separate appearances in *The Adventures of Huckleberry Finn*, performing perfectly its job as a key actor in the film.

　　Shooting wrapped up late in January of 1939. A separate film crew had already traveled to Alabama to shoot background footage and scenery, and Frank Waxman's original music for the film was recorded. Expert MGM film editor Frank Hall put the final pieces of the puzzle together and *The Adventures of Huckleberry Finn* was ready to roll.

Huck Hits the Screen

When Rooney saw the trailer for the film, he must have realized he was a long way from shedding his Andy Hardy image. The trailer opens with a clip of Rooney clowning as Andy Hardy and over his image are superimposed the words "The Hero of the Hardy Family." MGM apparently wanted to make sure audiences understood that Huck Finn would be played by Andy Hardy! *The Adventures of Huckleberry Finn* was distributed nationally by Loew's in the early spring of 1939, and it opened as a major film in theaters throughout the country. The *New York Times* gave it a generally poor review, lamenting what scriptwriter Hugo Butler had done to Twain's story and claiming Rooney was miscast. *Newsweek* magazine was kinder: "If *The Adventures of Huckleberry Finn* fails to capture the real flavor of Mark Twain's time on the Mississippi, it does succeed in blending reliable screen ingredients into colorful and palatable entertainment." Local critics were far more enthusiastic, giving it almost universal praise for Rooney's performance and recommending it for family viewing.

As MGM management had predicted, audiences loved *The Adventures of Huckleberry Finn* and, as usual, they loved Mickey Rooney. The film was profitable on its first run, made somewhat easier by the fact Mickey was paid what, even then, seemed like a paltry $5,000. The movie's success did, however, continue Rooney's upward trajectory into filmdom's stratosphere. Before the year was out, Rooney was named movieland's most popular star and its biggest box office attraction. More than 70 percent of all MGM's profits that year came from Mickey Rooney films.

The presentation of *The Adventures of Huckleberry Finn* of 1939 was not a great movie, but it was certainly a memorable film. Its popularity with audiences and viewers has continued undiminished over the decades. It is regularly featured in 1930s film retrospectives, and it continues to be shown on television—while ten other film versions of the Twain story have faded from memory. After more than seven decades, the face of Mickey Rooney is still the quintessential image of Huckleberry Finn.

The *Delta Queen* riverboat

AFTER THE ADVENTURES OF HUCKLEBERRY FINN

The publication of this novel in 1885 put a final stamp on Twain's recognition as America's greatest writer. Other literary successes followed: *A Connecticut Yankee in King Arthur's Court*, *The American Claimant*, *The Tragedy of Puddinhead Wilson*, *Tom Sawyer, Detective*, and the story "A Horse's Tale." Unfortunately, Twain was not a genius at everything. He was a spendthrift and a poor businessman, and he eventually went bankrupt. To recoup his fortunes, Twain embarked on an extensive and grueling world lecture tour, eventually managing to repay all of his debtors. He retired to New York, where he lived out his days receiving fame and honors. He died in 1910 at the age of 71. Incredibly, Twain died just as he was born—with Halley's Comet streaking the night sky.

✻ ✻ ✻

The success of *The Adventures of Huckleberry Finn* kept Mickey Rooney's star on the rise. All through the 1940s, he was the most popular actor in films and the industry's top theater attraction. Rooney would go on to an entertainment career that spanned nine decades. He made more than eighty movies, starred in his own television show, and made innumerable stage appearances in America and abroad. Over the years, he became celebrated for his eight marriages. (When seventeen-year-old Leslie Caron left Paris to make her first film in Hollywood, her mother admonished her, "Now, don't marry Mickey Rooney!") Rooney has four stars on the "Hollywood Walk of Fame" and in 2009 he was named by industry associates as a "A National Treasure."

✻ ✻ ✻

Walter Connolly followed his role as "The King" by costarring in six more films in 1939. He died unexpectedly the next year at the age of 53.

✻ ✻ ✻

William Frawley, "The Duke," continued his successful movie career as a character actor and had a major role in the legendary *Miracle on 34th Street*. He achieved lasting fame with his role of Fred Mertz in the *I Love Lucy* television series and by playing the grandfather in the Fred MacMurray series *My Three Sons*. Frawley died in 1966, having appeared in more than a hundred movies.

✻ ✻ ✻

Hugo Butler went on to achieve a full and creditable Hollywood career—writing more than thirty movies and winning an Academy Award nomination for *Edison, the Man*. During the 1950s, he was blacklisted by the industry for his communist activities but continued to work under an assumed name. After his death in 1968, the Writers Guild of America voted to give him posthumous and official credit for all of his screen work.

✻ ✻ ✻

The *Delta Queen* continued in passenger service on the Sacramento River for less than a year after her starring role in *The Adventures of Huckleberry Finn*. She was put into military service with the U.S. Navy during World War II and then was transported to New Orleans, where she became a real Mississippi riverboat, carrying as many as four hundred passengers between Cincinnati and her homeport for over half a century. The *Delta Queen* is now permanently docked in Chattanooga, Tennessee, and is listed as a National Historic Monument.

Max Baer, despite working out with Mickey Rooney during the filming of *The Adventures of Huckleberry Finn*, lost his championship bout to Lou Nova on June 1, 1939.

Poster for *The Adventures of Huckleberry Finn*

The Adventures of Huckleberry Finn
The Final Facts

Studio:	Metro-Goldwyn-Mayer
Producer:	Joseph L. Mankiewicz
Director:	Richard Thorpe
Screenplay:	Hugo Butler
Original Story:	Mark Twain
Photographer:	John F. Seltz
Release Date:	February 10, 1939
Running Time:	92 minutes
Cost of Production:	Unrecorded
Box Office:	Unknown, but considered profitable to the studio

Cast

Huckleberry Finn	Mickey Rooney
Jim	Rex Ingram
The King	Walter Connolly
The Duke	William Frawley
Mary Jane	Lynne Carver
Susan	Jo Ann Sayers
Captain Brandy	Minor Watson
Pap Finn	Victor Kilian
Miss Watson	Clara Blandick
Widow Douglas	Elisabeth Risdon

Awards
None—but considered the best and most popular
of almost a dozen Huckleberry Finn films.

First edition of *The Wonderful Wizard of Oz*

THE WIZARD OF OZ

THE STORY

Sunday mornings were always a special time for L. Frank Baum because he knew the children would gather around him to hear a story. But this Sunday, he first had to finish reading his *Chicago Tribune* because the news was important: Admiral Dewey had accomplished a great military victory in Manila and it would be a date to remember: May 7, 1898. When he finally finished reading the paper, he put it aside and let the children into the den. In addition to his son, Frank Jr., and his three brothers, there were three neighborhood children in the group. Some sat in chairs, others spread out on the floor, all waiting for the start of another tale. It had been that way for as many Sundays as they could remember, and they were seldom disappointed.

L. Frank Baum

Before he began, Baum picked up a pencil and put his writing pad on his knee so he could make notes as he talked. He leaned back in his big leather upholstered chair and began— not quite where he had left off—but close enough so that no one objected. It was a story he had been telling and embellishing for a long time now, a story about a little girl who found herself in a strange land, accompanied by two men, one made of straw and another made of tin. They were searching for an emerald city where everything was green, even the sky, and where hope resided. There were always obstacles on the way—witches and flying monkeys and impenetrable forests. Sometimes there were poisonous flowers, and once there was a cow that gave ice cream. Sometimes the name of the little girl changed, but today it was Dorothy, and she had a little dog named Toto, and they were lost in a strange fairyland.

The children would often interrupt to ask a question. What was the name of the good witch? When was Dorothy going to be home again? This morning, one of them asked a question several of them had wondered about: What was the name of this strange land? Baum didn't have a quick answer, but then he happened to glance over at his filing cabinet. The top drawer was labeled "A-N." The bottom cabinet said "O-Z." "Why," he said, "this story took place in a land called 'Oz'!"

Baum at his writing desk

Frank Baum had been writing and telling stories most of his life. As a youngster growing up in a small village outside Syracuse, New York, he was known as a daydreamer—always reading, writing poetry, and telling tall tales to his friends. He never lacked for an audience: He was the seventh of nine children in a prosperous Methodist family. When he was barely a teenager, his father gave him a small printing press, and he began publishing his own little newspaper for which he wrote articles and stories. Baum loved the theater, never missing a chance to see a traveling show or an amateur entertainment.

Baum also possessed a strong entrepreneurial streak. At the age of twenty, he began breeding fancy poultry—and he then wrote a book about the experience. He would later be a retail shop owner, a traveling salesman, and a shop window designer—and, of course, he wrote books about those experiences as well. He also started a minor league baseball team—which resulted in neither profits nor a book.

While Baum had the entrepreneurial spirit, he unfortunately did not have business acumen. He repeatedly failed in business and, because he was now married and raising a family, he decided he should try to make his way in literature and in the theater. He had already written a number of plays and had founded his own small theatrical production company. Like so many of his other projects, they were financial failures. In 1897, he wrote and published a collection of Mother Goose stories, using his proper name, L. Frank Baum. The collection was illustrated by an aspiring artist named Maxfield Parrish, and the book was successful enough that Baum decided to devote himself full-time to writing.

The Road to Oz

A mutual friend introduced Baum to a resident artist named William Wallace Denslow, who was already an established figure in the art world of Chicago. Denslow had a reputation as a newspaper artist and as a designer of posters and of book covers. He had a knack for portraying whimsical and fantastical subjects. Baum and Denslow became fast friends and it was only a matter of time before they decided to collaborate. Baum wanted to capitalize on the success of his Mother Goose book with a series of tales called *Father Goose*. The two of them worked on the book together, with Baum's prose inspiring Denslow and Denslow's drawings inspiring Baum. The combination produced a beautiful and enchanting book, and it also produced a lasting partnership between the writer and the artist in which they agreed to share both credit and royalties. *Father Goose* was even more successful than its predecessor.

Denslow with one of his drawings

Published in 1899, it sold more than twenty-five thousand copies before the year was out. The partnership was off to a great start.

By this time, Baum had developed a custom of entertaining his children and their friends with his fanciful tales. This served two purposes. Baum loved to entertain and to be the center of attention, and he found his gatherings with young people fulfilling and satisfying. But it also permitted Baum to see what kind of stories they most enjoyed. He learned that they were not keen on stories that pointed up a moral or taught a lesson. He saw that their minds wandered off and their attention flagged at the first hint of romance or of tales about princes and princesses. They liked child heroes, unexpected happenings, scary situations, and magical escapes. Over time, it became obvious to Baum that the children were especially fond of the story he had created and embellished about the little girl Dorothy who found herself in a strange and scary world populated by witches, a tin woodsman, and a scarecrow. He invented a green city for them and a wizard. He knew from their interest and their reactions that he was onto something good. He decided to ask his friend and partner William Denslow to see what he could contribute to the story, which he now called "The Emerald City."

In the summer of 1899, Denslow joined Baum in his writer's den and Baum outlined for him the story that he had been telling the children off and on for two years. Baum leaned back in his leather chair as he talked and puffed on his cigar as he wrote on his pad with a soft lead pencil. While he talked, Denslow sketched on his own pad, puffing on his pipe. Over the days that followed, through the smoke and conversation, the characters came to life in word and picture—Dorothy, the Good Witch of the North, the Wicked Witch of the West, the dog Toto, the Tin Woodsman, the Scarecrow, and the Wizard. Then Denslow drew something new: a Cowardly Lion. Baum loved it and they put him into the story. Baum wrote in such a careful hand that the publisher could set type from it. Denslow's drawings showed comic animals with human features and were executed with distinctive color tones. Baum had been calling his unfolding story "The Emerald City," but now he decided that

Denslow's drawing
of the Cowardly Lion

title was not sufficiently descriptive of the expanded novel, so he changed it to *From Kansas to Fairyland*.

The book had no problem finding a publisher. George H. Hill, who had published their *Father Goose* book, paid a $500 advance to both Baum and Denslow and agreed to pay 12 percent royalty payments on a list price of $1.50 per copy. Hill also told Baum he didn't like the title *From Kansas to Fairyland*. Baum countered with *The Land of Oz*, and the book was copyrighted under that title. However, neither Denslow nor Hill were happy with the new title, so Baum came up with one more try. In September of 1900, the book that they finally published was entitled *The Wonderful Wizard of Oz*.

The book was an immediate success. It was reviewed by more than two hundred newspapers and periodicals. Superlatives danced through almost every review: "delightful humor and rare philosophy found on every page"…"Dorothy's companions are both real and wonderful"…"new features and ideals of fairy life"…"ingeniously woven out of commonplace material"…"philosophy and satire that will furnish amusement to the adult and cause the juvenile to think some new and healthy thoughts."

As Christmastime approached, the Baum household was short of funds, so Baum was asked by his wife to go to his publisher's office to see if he could possibly collect a hundred or so dollars in royalties. Reluctantly, he did as he was asked. He came home and handed his wife the sealed envelope he had been given. When she opened the envelope and pulled out the enclosure, she gasped in astonishment. Together, they looked at it in disbelief. It was a check for $3,432.64.

Before the next year was out, *The Wonderful Wizard of Oz* had sold more than thirty-seven thousand copies and had become the best-selling children's book in America.

Baum took advantage of the great success of *The Wonderful Wizard of Oz* by indulging his great love of the theater. He mounted a stage version of the book using, for the first time, the title by which his creation would eventually be known—*The Wizard of Oz*. The show ran successfully on Broadway and then toured the United States off and on over the next ten years. Baum also capitalized on the reception of the original book by writing sixteen more "Oz" books. His later "Oz" efforts varied in quality, although most were well received by his readers.

Over the remainder of his life, Baum continued his prolific writing career, publishing dozens of novels, short stories, and plays under his own name and using various pseudonyms. He moved to Hollywood and became involved in motion pictures, starting his own movie company, called The Oz Film Manufacturing Company. But once again his business sense failed him. He announced that he was purchasing an island off the West Coast with the purpose of turning it into an Oz fairyland, and he invested in a number of unsuccessful films and theater projects. In 1914, Baum was forced to declare bankruptcy.

Despite his personal and financial problems, Baum continued to write until his death from a heart attack in 1919 at the age of sixty-two. His final Oz book, *Glinda of Oz*, was published posthumously. Other authors, licensed to continue the series by his estate, subsequently published an additional nineteen "Oz" books.

Various editions and adventures in Oz

"OZ" GOES TO THE MOVIES

In 1925, a quarter of a century after the publication of *The Wonderful Wizard of Oz*, L. Frank Baum Jr., Baum's eldest son and inheritor of the Oz mantle, became involved with filmmaker Larry Semon and the two produced a silent film version of *The Wizard of Oz*. It is mostly memorable in that it involved a young Oliver Hardy in the role of the Scarecrow. The film took considerable liberties with Baum's original plot. Dorothy's three traveling companions were all portrayed as the same Kansas farmhands in various disguises. Dorothy became a young seductress involved in a love triangle with two of the other farmhands. Mercifully, the producing studio, Chadwick Pictures, went bankrupt before the movie had gone into full distribution and the film is all but forgotten.

Nine years later, movie mogul Sam Goldwyn purchased the film rights for *The Wonderful Wizard of Oz* from the Baum estate for $40,000. Goldwyn's planned to star bug-eyed singer-dancer Eddy Cantor in the film but, for some reason lost to history, the project fell through. It was with a sense of relief that Goldwyn managed to turn a profit by reselling the film rights to MGM in early 1938 for $75,000. Louis B. Mayer, head of the MGM studio, was never one to let an asset lie idle. He quickly assigned the property to one of his top producers, Mervyn LeRoy, for development.

LeRoy, at age thirty-eight, was a Hollywood phenomenon. He had already directed forty motion pictures for Warner Brothers when Mayer hired him to produce films for MGM. In the depths of the Depression, LeRoy was signed at the extraordinary salary of $6,000 a week and was told to make money for the studio. His first picture would be *The Wizard of Oz,* and he needed to get off to a good start. His first task was to take the Baum story and turn it into a filmable movie script.

Mervyn LeRoy

The Writer Rolodex

The scriptwriting assignment went to Herman Mankiewicz. Mankiewicz was MGM's resident genius at turning out superb and moneymaking scripts—and for getting them done fast. Hardworking but easily bored, he tended to work night and day on an assignment for fear of losing interest if he allowed himself too much time. True to his reputation, Mankiewicz quickly turned in a seventeen-page overall treatment in which he recommended that the opening and closing scenes be shot in black and white and that the scenes in Oz be filmed in color. It was an idea that was quickly accepted and that would become a legendary aspect of the movie. In another four-day burst of creativity, he finished a fifty-six-page script for the entire movie.

However, given the accepted way of doing things at MGM, it was just a start.

Within days, LeRoy gave identical assignments to writers Ogden Nash and Noel Langley: Come up with a script for "Oz." None of the three writers had any idea that others were also on the job. Nash made a few script suggestions but largely fanned on the assignment. Langley, on the other hand, charged into the task with a fury of creativity. In less than a week, he gave LeRoy a full forty-three-page treatment that would eventually serve as the outline for the final script—and then Mankiewicz took over again and followed up quickly with a full and

Writer Noel Langley

detailed shooting script. But that did not mean that MGM writers were permitted to rest. Before a script was finally certified, eleven different scriptwriters were asked to take a shot at *The Wizard of Oz*. The script remained a work-in-progress almost until the final scene was shot. Yet, when all was said and done, and LeRoy had to determine the credits, it was Langley who survived. The film was credited as "treatment by Noel Langley" and, additionally, Langley was named as one of three contributing writers. Noel Langley, however, eventually disavowed his work on "Oz" because of all the changes that were later made. When he finally saw the finished film months later, he was so angry that he wept.

THE MOVIE SCRIPT FOR *THE WIZARD OF OZ*

The film opens in black and white. Dorothy, a pretty young Kansas farm girl, and her dog Toto live with her Auntie Em and Uncle Henry. Dorothy is concerned about Toto because he is being threatened by an evil neighbor lady called Miss Gulch who claims the dog has uprooted her vegetables. Dorothy soothes her concerns by singing a sentimental song. Armed with a sheriff's order, Miss Gulch takes Toto away in a basket on her bike. The dog manages to escape and returns home where a fearful Dorothy takes Toto and runs away. On her journey, she comes across Professor Marvel, an idiosyncratic traveling showman, who convinces her to return home.

Back at the farm, there is a sudden and fierce tornado which transports Dorothy and Toto into an incredible new fantasy world. As the film goes from black and white to vivid color, Dorothy says, "Toto, I have a feeling we're not in Kansas anymore."

Dorothy is suddenly surrounded by little people called "Munchkins." They sing a welcoming song. It turns out that the airborne farmhouse that carried Dorothy to Oz has landed on the Wicked Witch of the East and has killed her. The Munchkins and Glinda, the Good Witch, celebrate by singing a song, and then they proclaim Dorothy their heroine. Suddenly, the Wicked Witch of the West, recognizable as Miss Gulch from the earlier sequence, arrives and declares Dorothy her enemy. She also demands the ruby slippers which Dorothy is now wearing, but finds they cannot be removed. The witch threatens Dorothy again and disappears in a cloud of smoke.

Dorothy tells Glinda that she only wants to go home, and Glinda tells her that there is a strange and powerful Wizard of Oz in the Emerald City who can help her and that she must follow the Yellow Brick Road to find him. Dorothy begins her journey, singing a song about the road that she must travel. At a division in the road, she encounters a Scarecrow, which she rescues from his perch. The Scarecrow says he has no brain and so cannot really scare anyone. Dorothy invites him to join her on her way to see the all-powerful Wizard. The Scarecrow celebrates by singing and dancing a song about jitterbugs. Then they proceed together, singing about their goal of seeing the Wizard.

On their journey, they discover a Tin Woodsman, who is so rusted he cannot move. Dorothy rescues him with an oil can and he sings a song of gratitude. After he tells Dorothy he has no heart, she invites him to join them on their way to find the Wizard. Together, they proceed down the Yellow Brick Road, singing their way along.

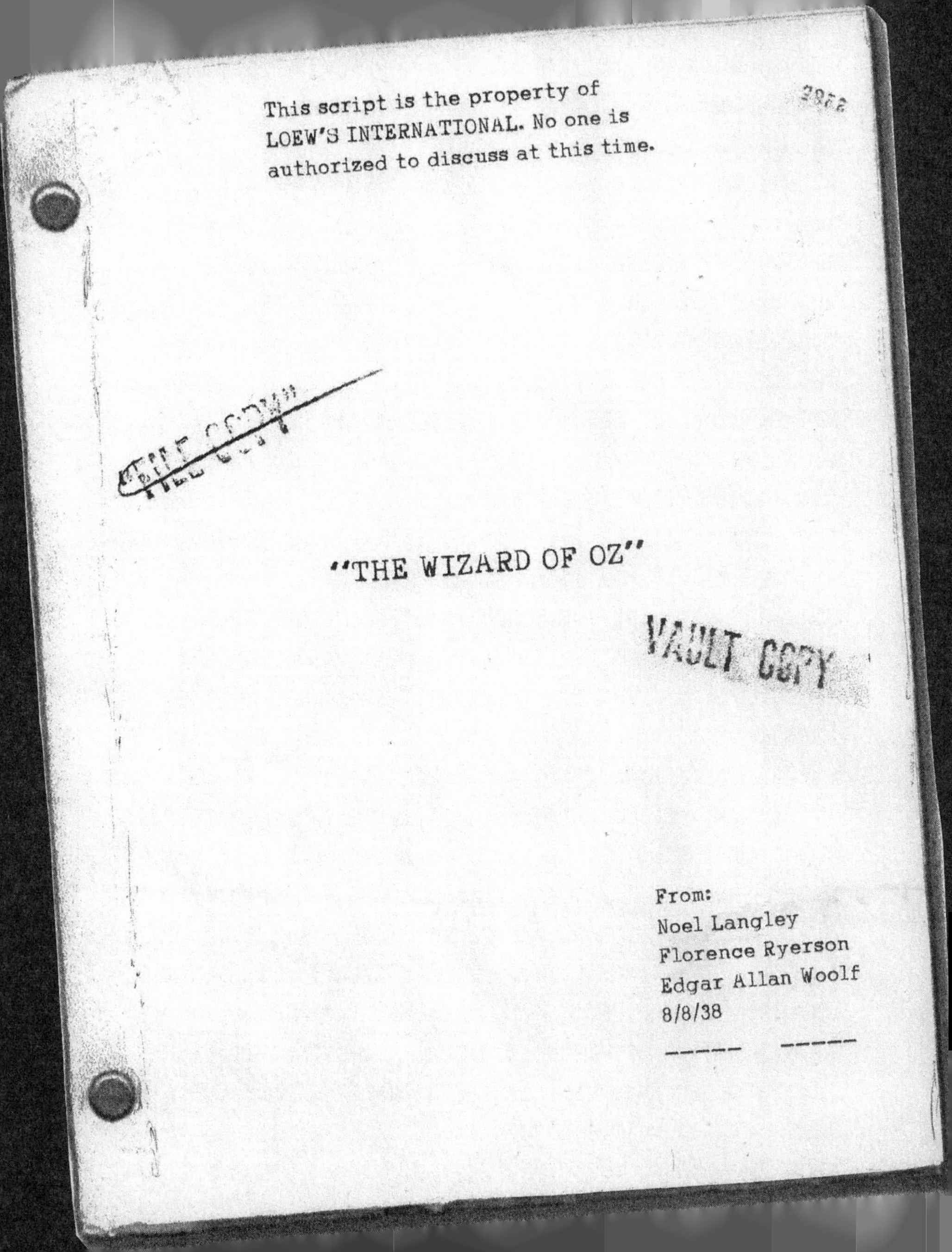

This script is the property of
LOEW'S INTERNATIONAL. No one is
authorized to discuss at this time.

"FILE COPY"

"THE WIZARD OF OZ"

VAULT COPY

From:
Noel Langley
Florence Ryerson
Edgar Allan Woolf
8/8/38

As they travel through a scary forest, they come across a Cowardly Lion, who sings a song, confessing that he has no courage. Dorothy tells him of the Wizard and invites him to join in their quest for the powerful man who will solve all their problems. The Cowardly Lion joins them as they journey on in song.

The Wicked Witch now reappears and, in an effort to thwart the three travelers, makes them lie down in a field of poppies that will put them into a lasting sleep. However, the Good Witch produces a magical snowfall which revives them. They proceed on, singing their way toward the Emerald City. Dorothy and her companions finally enter the Emerald City and are granted an audience with the mighty Wizard, who greets them with explosions of smoke and fire. He announces that all their wishes will be granted but that they must first leave and bring back the broomstick of the Wicked Witch.

The Wicked Witch, however, is determined to get Dorothy's ruby slippers and unleashes her horde of ugly flying monkeys to snatch Dorothy and Toto and bring them to her castle. The monkeys are successful, but the Wicked Witch discovers the slippers cannot be removed from Dorothy's feet. In frustration, she condemns Dorothy to death and displays an hourglass whose dripping sands will determine how long she has to live.

Toto escapes from the castle, finds the Scarecrow, the Tin Woodsman, and the Cowardly Lion and leads them back to the castle. There, disguised as guards, they attempt to rescue Dorothy. When the Wicked Witch foils them and sets the Scarecrow on fire, Dorothy finds a pail of water and extinguishes the flames on her friend; but she also inadvertently splashes water on the Wicked Witch. The water melts the Wicked Witch, who dissolves and disappears. The Wicked Witch's subjects, delighted to have their evil leader gone, rejoice and hail Dorothy as their savior. In their gratitude, they award her the Wicked Witch's broomstick.

Dorothy and her three companions return to the Emerald City and show the Wicked Witch's broomstick to the Wizard. He tells them that he appreciates their gift but that they will have to come back the next day before he can grant any favors. Dorothy is enraged at this betrayal and, while she argues with the Wizard, Toto runs over and pulls aside a curtain revealing that the Wizard is actually a mere mortal, recognizable as the traveling professor from the opening sequence of the movie. The Wizard recovers from his embarrassment and attempts to fulfill his promises. He gives the Scarecrow an elaborate diploma and pronounces him "a doctor of thinkology." He confers a medal on the Cowardly Lion and makes him a member of the "Legion of Courage." He pins a ticking heart on the Tin Woodsman and tells him it represents real love. He then informs Dorothy that he is about to leave for Kansas in a hot air balloon and promises to take her with him. When Dorothy chases after Toto, she misses the balloon flight and is left stranded in the Emerald City.

Glinda, the Good Witch, suddenly appears on the scene and informs Dorothy that she had possessed the power to return to Kansas all along. All she needs to do is click her magical ruby slippers together and say, "There's no place like home!" When Dorothy follows her instructions, she suddenly wakes up in her own black-and-white world back in Kansas, in bed and surrounded by Auntie Em and Uncle Henry, by three farmhands whom she recognizes as her Oz traveling companions, and by the professor, who looks exactly like the Wizard. They explain to her that she was rendered unconscious by the tornado and that she must have been dreaming. With Toto in her arms, she proclaims again that there is truly "no place like home."

THE END

The shooting script differed from the Baum novel in a number of ways. Most important, Dorothy was given an altered persona. She was older than the girl in the book, and she was portrayed as a damsel-in-distress, needing her new companions to survive. Baum's Dorothy, on the contrary, was a girl in firm command, feisty and determined to solve her own problems, using her intelligence and determination.

The Wicked Witch is a relatively minor figure in the original story, involved in only a few scenes in which she torments Dorothy. In the movie, the Wicked Witch is an ever-present source of apprehension

Dorothy and her new friends
sing their way to Oz.

and the source of evil that must be vanquished. Several of Baum's memorable characters—the Hummingbirds and the Hammerheads—were eliminated in the interests of plot flow and the restrictions of time. And, happily for posterity, Dorothy's magical silver shoes where changed to ruby red slippers.

Perhaps the most significant change, and the one that accounts for the success and popularity of the movie, was the invention of the dream concept. In the original novel, Oz is a real place and all of its inhabitants and all locations actually exist. This made the story extremely vivid and frightening for Baum's young readers. In Baum's book, for instance, Dorothy's farmhouse is completely destroyed in the tornado so she has no place in which to return. In the movie, we know from the outset that Dorothy is in a fanciful place, that she is dreaming the story, that the dangers will all dissipate, and that Dorothy will somehow get back home to Kansas. Oz is clearly a fairyland and not an alternative universe—and this adds to the pleasure and enjoyment of the movie.

Critics have counted almost fifty ways in which the movie departs from the novel, and yet the film script managed to retain the essence and flavor of Baum's work. Dorothy, the Scarecrow, the Tin Man, the Cowardly Lion, the Good Witch, the Wicked Witch, and the Wizard all remain essentially intact and their overall adventure is faithful to the original plot. Even little Toto plays his role, for the most part, just as Baum wrote it.

FINDING DOROTHY

In the late 1930s, MGM had an amazing galaxy of stars under exclusive contract. There were more than 130 in all, including Clark Gable, Joan Crawford, Greta Garbo, Spencer Tracy, William Powell, Myrna Loy, Judy Garland, Hedy Lamarr, Mickey Rooney, Basil Rathbone, Helen Hayes, Wallace Beery, Jimmy Stewart, Deanna Durbin, and Freddie Bartholomew, as well as a host of child and juvenile actors.

With all this star power, the moguls of MGM decided they had to look elsewhere for their Dorothy. They wanted someone with a history of filling up theater seats. They wanted box office insurance. They wanted Shirley Temple.

Temple was at the peak of her young career. Ever since her breakout performance in *Stand Up and Cheer* in 1934, she had been dazzling theatergoers with her winsome, dimpled charm and her delightful singing and dancing. She was considered Hollywood's number-one star in 1935, 1936, and 1937. She was now ten years old, older than Dorothy had been portrayed in Baum's story, but she was, in a sense, timeless. She was simply America's darling. Under contract to rival studio Twentieth Century Fox, Temple would command a high price as a loan-out, but Louis B.

Shirley Temple

Mayer was determined. Negotiations, however, were difficult. Temple was currently filming *Rebecca of Sunnybrook Farm* and was already scheduled for other upcoming films, including *The Little Princess* and *Little Miss Broadway*. In addition, Darryl Zanuck wasn't about to give up his little gold mine to his main competitor. After a few weeks of negotiations, it became clear that MGM would have to take another look at its own roster.

LOOKING FOR THEIR STAR AT MGM

Judy Garland stood out like a beacon of hope. At age sixteen, she seemed much too old for the role of Dorothy, but she had some talents that could compensate. She had a nice, comfortable, Midwestern look, which would be ideal for Dorothy, the Kansas farm girl. With the proper clothes, makeup, and body shaping, she could be made to look younger. More important, she had the best singing voice in Hollywood.

Garland had started singing early in life. The daughter of two vaudevillians, she was on stage before she was ten, performing as part of a trio with her two older sisters. They toured the vaudeville circuit for several years as the Gumm Sisters, with young Frances Gumm

The Gumm Sisters

(Garland's real name) as the lead singer. In 1934, the girls played the Oriental Theater in Chicago with star George Jessel. Jessel convinced the sisters that Gumm was not a good show business name and suggested Garland as an alternative. Frances Gumm decided that while she was at it, she would also change her first name to that of the name of a currently popular Hoagy Carmichael song. From that point on she was Judy Garland.

The trio broke up a year later when the oldest sister married, and Judy began working as a single, performing in the theaters and clubs. Everyone who heard her agreed that she had a truly remarkable voice. One agent was so impressed that he arranged a personal audition for Judy in Louis B. Mayer's office. At the age of thirteen, she was signed to an exclusive movie contract by the biggest studio in Hollywood.

As talented as she was, Garland presented problems as a movie performer. She was at an awkward age, too old for child roles and too young for more mature parts as a teenager. Not even five feet tall, Judy did not have the look of a movie star. Her face was flawed, her teeth were random, and her body was pudgy and awkward. She was regarded by the studio as a phenomenal talent locked up inside an inadequate package. As she grew older, MGM would reshape her nose, straighten her teeth, pluck her eyebrows, and do its best to remold her body. Even so, Mayer would frequently refer to her ungallantly as "my little hunchback." Still, in the end, the talent, the voice, and the look of adolescent innocence would enable her to triumph over her shortcomings.

Judy was put to work in a succession of lesser movies that capitalized on her singing and on her appearance as a somewhat awkward youngster. In her first two years at MGM, she appeared in six films, most memorably as a love-struck youngster singing "Dear Mr. Gable," while holding a picture of the studio's biggest star. In 1938, she enhanced her standing with theatergoers as the love interest to Mickey Rooney in *Love Finds Andy Hardy*. On February 24 of that year, *Variety*, the industry bible, announced

Young Judy Garland

that Judy Garland had been cast by Metro-Goldwyn-Mayer to play the role of Dorothy in the upcoming film production of *The Wizard of Oz*.

MAKING "OZ" SING

It was understood from the outset that *The Wizard of Oz* would be a musical in the grand MGM sense of the word. And now, with the voice of Judy Garland at the team's disposal, the musical opportunities were dramatically enhanced. Arthur Freed, named by LeRoy as the assistant producer on the film, had a special talent for coaxing superior music out of MGM's composers and lyricists. Freed, who had already made his musical mark on such films as *Dancing Lady*, *A Night at the Opera*, and *Broadway Melody*, took on the "Oz" assignment with relish, recognizing that it was an opportunity to solidify his reputation in the movie industry.

Freed selected the songwriting team of composer Harold Arlen and lyricist E. Y. (Yip) Harburg for the "Oz" project. The two already had a track record on both Broadway and in Hollywood, having created songs for earlier films: *The Singing Kid*, *Stage Stuck*, and *Gold Diggers of 1937*. They had recently had a Broadway hit with *Hooray for What!* Arlen and Harburg recognized that "Oz" presented a unique opportunity to

Arlen and Harburg

create songs that were integrated into the plot and that advanced the action of the film. They also knew that in Judy Garland they had a remarkable singer with an unusual vocal range. Working with Langley's screen treatment, they set about creating songs for Dorothy and each of her three traveling companions. Most of the time, they worked at night because Arlen was such an avid golfer that he insisted on hitting the links almost every day.

The first songs they composed were the "action songs": "Ding Dong! The Witch Is Dead" and "We're Off to See the Wizard." Then came the songs that would establish the Scarecrow ("If I Only Had a Brain"), the Tin Woodsman ("If...a Heart"), and the Cowardly Lion ("If...the Nerve"). Finally, they turned their attentions to what they knew would be the key song in the movie: a ballad to dramatize Dorothy's yearning for a better life. After a number of tries, Arlen came up with a soaring melody line and Harburg was able to find the right words that fit the music and that captured Dorothy's sense of longing. The result was "Over the Rainbow" and, perfect as it was for its place in the film, they would have to fight over and over with the authorities at MGM for its inclusion in the film.

FINDING THE WIZARD

The role of the Wizard required an unusual acting personality. The Wizard was a con man, a bumbler, a humbug. It required an experienced actor, preferably known to theater audiences, who could play it with broad humor, yet with a certain rogue majesty. Producer LeRoy and his casting head soon developed a very short list of options: Ed Wynn and W. C. Fields. Screenwriter Langley was so keen on Fields and so certain that he would accept the role that he wrote the part of the Wizard with Fields in mind. But others were high on Ed Wynn, whose quavering voice and fussy mannerisms seemed tailormade for the role. Wynn had appeared in a few films, but his reputation was as a stage comedian and comic writer, and he seemed fearful of jeopardizing his stage reputation in what he considered a rival medium. He also valued his reputation as a star and had turned down more than one film offer in which he would not receive top billing. Additionally, he was extremely busy with current commitments. There was disappointment but not surprise when he turned down MGM's offer to play the Wizard.

The production team's enthusiasm was quickly transferred to W. C. Fields. Fields had all the equipment needed to be a great Wizard—a great comic look, a sardonic attitude, wonderful pomposity, and a knack for dominating the screen with his comic presence. Audiences loved him. He would play the character with more bluff, wit, and bombast than Wynn and that was fine with the director. But Fields was not an MGM property. Interestingly enough, in a world of more or less indentured movie actors, he was very much his own man, making pictures for both Paramount and Universal, often writing his own material, frequently railing at the studio bosses. His role as Mr.

W. C. Fields

Micawber in David Selznick's *David Copperfield* had established him as an important actor, as well as a comedian. Producer LeRoy knew that Field's drawing power at the nation's theaters could be another guarantee of success for "Oz." He offered Fields an extraordinary salary to take the role: $75,000. When contrasted with Judy Garland's $500 a week salary, it seems like a veritable fortune. Fields was interested but thought

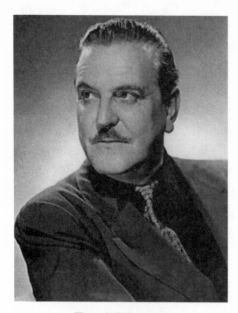

Frank Morgan

the offer inadequate. He wanted $100,000. LeRoy despaired and decided to look elsewhere. While they were searching the actor's roster to see whom to court next, an actor they hadn't even thought about began to court them.

Frank Morgan was a veteran film performer with more than fifty films and one Academy Award nomination on his résumé. Morgan specialized in playing middle-aged men who were befuddled and goodhearted and, when he heard that the role of the Wizard might be open, he sensed it was an assignment he could take on with zest. He called on some friends at MGM and begged for an audition. With nothing to lose, the studio agreed and Morgan went on a studio stage by himself, with no supporting actors. He put on a dazzling test performance. The same actor would be playing Professor Marvel, the carriage driver of "A Horse of a Different Color," the Wizard, and the disembodied head of the Wizard in the frightening apparition scene. With no script to guide him, Morgan ad-libbed all the roles alone on stage. When the director saw the test film later, he was bowled over. The search ended on September 22, 1938. Frank Morgan was signed to play the Wizard of Oz.

THE SEARCH FOR DOROTHY'S COMPANIONS

Casting Dorothy's accidental companions who journey with her on the road to Oz was critical to the film's success. Fortunately, however, this did not seem to present any major problems. The first choice for the role of the Cowardly Lion was Bert Lahr. Lahr was a veteran vaudevillian and stage performer who combined a comical demeanor with a kind of innate sweetness in his appearance and manner. He had not been especially successful in films because, like so many stage actors, his acting style was broad and his gestures were magnified to appeal to live theater audiences. Still, he seemed tailormade for the heavily costumed Cowardly Lion and MGM offered him three weeks of work on the film for $7,500. Lahr read the script and was keen to do the role, but asked for a five-week guarantee. A month of negotiations got him the deal he wanted—although, as it turned out, he would spend six months on the "Oz" set.

In March of 1938, producer LeRoy summoned contract player Ray Bolger to his office for a meeting. Bolger, famed for his athletic and fluid dancing style, suspected it would be an assignment on the "Oz" film. He had read the script and was confident he could handle the role of the Scarecrow. It was exactly the kind of part he had trained for all his life. He was only partly right. He would be doing the "Oz" movie, but he would be playing the Tin Man, a role in which all his movements would be mechanical and stilted. He sputtered his astonishment, but it made no difference. He would be encased in tin. The $3,000 a week offer provided Bolger some solace.

Burt Lahr

Ray Bolger

The role coveted by Bolger went to actor-dancer Buddy Ebsen. Ebsen was tall and thin and knew his way around the floorboards. Three years into his contract with MGM,

Billie Burke

he eagerly accepted the role of the Scarecrow. Not that he had much choice. As a minor star making half as much as Bolger, he did what he was told and went about practicing the fluid dance moves necessary to depicting a man made of straw.

FINDING THE WITCHES

Candidates for Glinda, the Good Witch, abounded. The list of contract actors capable of playing the part included Gracie Fields, Fannie Bruce, and Una Merkel. But the production team fastened quickly on Billie Burke, a celebrated Broadway star and a veteran movie actress with a pretty face, a winsome smile, and a charming voice. The widow of showman Florenz Ziegfeld, Burke seemed to have all the natural equipment to play a witch that theatergoers would cheer for. Still living in the shadow of a huge debt inherited from her famous husband, she eagerly signed on for the role.

MGM had two directions they could have taken to find their Wicked Witch. The immediate previous model for wicked witches was that from Disney's *Snow White*, in which the witch was beautiful and glamorous in appearance but evil in her tone and demeanor. The second option was to put on the screen a witch who was not only evil but looked the part. Producer LeRoy was inclined to the former and went about grooming contract player Gale Sondergaard for the role. An attractive and talented actress, she had recently won an Academy Award as Best Supporting Actress. But while she was in the midst of rehearsing the role, LeRoy was persuaded by his staff that a clear contrast with the good witch was required and that the Wicked Witch should look and sound wicked and hateful. One glance at the casting photo of Margaret Hamilton convinced LeRoy that she could do the job.

Hamilton was a veteran character actress who usually played maids or ancillary roles on stage and in film. She was no beauty, but she had character and talent, and in her interview she displayed a marvelous, chilling, cackling laugh. Hamilton wanted the job and the laugh sold LeRoy. However, there were budget problems, and MGM offered Hamilton a limited contract at $1,000 a week for three weeks work. Her agent wanted a six-

Margaret Hamilton

week guarantee and finally got it after some tough negotiations. As it turned out, Hamilton would spend more than four difficult months on the set before wrapping up her work as the Wicked Witch.

FINDING THE MUNCHKINS

MGM decided it needed at least a hundred little people—midgets and dwarfs—to populate the landscape of Oz. The possibility of using children was briefly discussed but was rejected because it was felt they wouldn't have the same look or demeanor that small adults would. Finding and signing hundreds of little people was a tall order.

MGM sought out Leo Singer, the proprietor of a group of performing small people called "Singer's Midgets." At one time, he had employed dozens of little people and little animals in a traveling show that featured comedy, acrobatics, magic, and feats of strength. With the advent of motion pictures and an economic recession, Singer's group had shrunk to eighteen, and he was eager to find a new source of revenue.

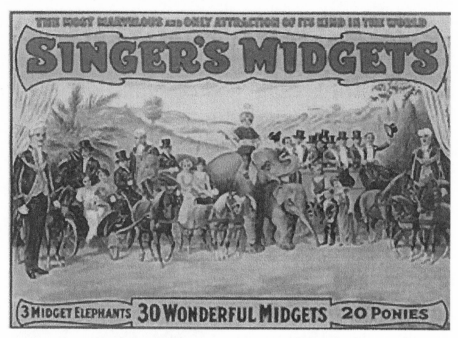

Singer's Midgets, source of the Munchkins

He signed on as the Munchkin casting director, left his own performing troupe with MGM as a starter set, and began scouring America for more little people. Midgets and dwarfs, many of them already in show business, soon got the word and headed for Hollywood. One busload of sixty midgets traveled all the way from the East Coast for their chance at fame. Small people were stopped on the street and signed up. The cost to MGM was not great: Most would make as little as fifty dollars a week during the filming. Within months, several prebooked hotels were teeming with little folk, strolling the halls, sitting in the lobbies, and filling the bars. For the other hotel patrons, it must have been an astonishing sight. Before the recruiting came to a close, Singer had signed almost a hundred of the required Munchkins, ranging in height from 2'6" tall to 4'5". MGM had to agree that Singer had delivered "big."

FINDING TOTO

The dog that would play Toto would be one of the most important actors in the film. He would be almost constantly at Dorothy's side, and would be the motivator of Miss Gulch's outrage, the companion of the quartet searching for the Wizard, the reason Dorothy misses the balloon flight, and the pioneer leading the way down the Yellow Brick Road. It would take a highly trained animal—and one that looked like the Toto readers had seen in Denslow's drawings in the original story.

Toto

There were a number of trainers in Hollywood who schooled their dogs for movie roles. Lee Duncan was celebrated for the skills he had installed in Rin Tin Tin. Rudd Weatherwax had made Lassie a household name. But it was trainer Carl Spitz who was sure he had the right dog under his tutelage.

The dog, Terry, was a frightened little creature that had been given to him for training three years earlier by her owner, a breeder from Pasadena. Terry's owner had despaired of the pretty, fine-coated terrier because of her shyness. Terry had recently spent three weeks under a bed, refusing to face the frightening world of humans. Spitz took Terry under his wing and nursed and nurtured her along until she was a confident little creature that obeyed simple commands and enjoyed life. Spitz figured his little pupil was ready for the big time and began searching for the right role for his canine protégé.

When the word went out that a dog was needed for "Oz," there was no specification as to breed. There was, however, a sketch of the illustration from the original "Oz" book. When Spitz saw the picture, he recognized immediately that Toto was a Cairn Terrier. He decided that Terry should try for an audition and, after rehearsing her in some simple commands that would be needed, he drove her over to the MGM studios. Spitz checked Terry in at the property department where she

Garland with the Munchkins on the set

passed muster, and he and Terry were then ushered into an office where the producer and the scriptwriter were at work. They took one look at Terry and gave an instant thumbs-up. On the assurance from Spitz that she was a reliable performer, they signed Terry on for the role of Toto. At $125 a week, she would be the lowest-paid principal actor on the set.

BUILDING OZ

The task of creating the sets for the Land of Oz and of costuming its hundreds of cast members presented awesome problems. The script required more than sixty sets, ranging from a simple farm bedroom to the grand, glittering Emerald City. Almost a thousand different costumes would have to be designed. Elaborate makeup designs would have to be created for the witches, the traveling quartet, and the Munchkins. The task was somewhat simplified by Denslow's drawings, which portrayed the principal characters and a number of the scenes in the original Baum story. MGM wanted to hew as close as possible to his drawings, knowing that many of the film's viewers had grown up with the book.

Munchkinland was designed and built to the scale of its inhabitants, with low doors and low-sitting flower boxes that were at a height where they could be watered by the little people. Houses with mushroom-shaped rooftops that were set in surroundings with bright colors and patterns gave the set a sense of other-worldly magic. Most sets consisted of constructed items in the foreground against painted backdrops. Many of the sets were done in miniature, including the Emerald City itself. Dorothy's farmhouse was actually only three feet tall. The glass ball in which the Good Witch is seen to arrive was in reality less than a foot in diameter. Matte paintings, used for a number of the scenes, were only about four feet high. An extraordinary number of artisans were involved in the creation of the sets, including more than five hundred carpenters and craftsmen and dozens of artists and painters. By the time everything was ready for filming, the *Wizard of Oz* set was spread over four complete stages on the MGM lot.

MAKING THE ACTORS LOOK THE PART

Terry was the only actor on the set who didn't require special costuming and makeup, although even she needed brushing and grooming before each shot to achieve Toto's cute, slightly frumpy look. Fortunately for MGM designers, they were able to follow Denslow's drawing for the Tin Woodsman (upside-down tin funnel hat, rivet buttons down the front), the Scarecrow (floppy hat, rope connecting head to body, straw protruding from neck, sleeves, and ankles), and the Cowardly Lion (furry hair and beard, long, tasseled tail). Dorothy was described in the book as dressed in "gingham with checks of white and blue," and so she was costumed in the movie.

The Munchkins presented a greater challenge. Eventually, there were 124 little people to be outfitted, all possessing different shapes and sizes and many playing special roles. Most of their costumes were designed with visible horizontal stripes to make them appear even shorter. Their final costumes were festooned with bows, bells, tassels, and flowers to add to their charm. Some of them would later appear in scenes at the Emerald City, where everyone was dressed in green— green hats, green jackets, green stockings, green pants, and even green shoes. MGM would spend a small fortune on green dye.

Only a few of the costumes were simply purchased on the open market. One of these exceptions was the coat for Frank Morgan in his role of Professor Marvel. In a quest for authenticity, the property department scoured used clothing stores and found a number of potential coats for Morgan to try on. After he selected one that fit properly, he looked into the inside pocket and found the name "L. Frank Baum." It seemed too much of a coincidence and a trick was suspected. But when the studio checked with the tailor who made the jacket, he confirmed that it had indeed been made for the author of *The Wonderful Wizard of Oz*.

WHAT COULD GO WRONG?

Even after all the careful planning that went into preproduction on this elaborate film, it was still inevitable that some things would go horribly wrong. And so they did. Filming began in October of 1938 and problems surfaced almost immediately. Ray Bolger, still unhappy at being cast as the Tin Woodsman, continued to badger the producer and director to play the Scarecrow, where he could utilize his unusual dancing skills. Even after costumes had been especially created for him as the Tin Woodsman and for Buddy Ebsen as the Scarecrow, Bolger continued his campaign. One day, while they were both in their last fittings, Bolger managed to convince Ebsen that they should change roles. When they went to LeRoy with their request, he threw up his hands in despair and approved the switch. It would prove to be a great move for Bolger, but a terrible one for Ebsen.

MGM knew that "Oz" would present some unique makeup problems, but the studio didn't foresee how massive they would be until the time came to get the actors ready for filming. Turning Lahr into the Cowardly Lion was a painful undertaking, and it took hours to achieve the transformation. A hair mask and beard were glued to his face, and his head was covered with a heavy fur wig. His body was encased in a heavy padded lion suit that weighed fifty pounds and made it difficult for him to move and dangerously heated up his body. He discovered that it was impossible for him to open his mouth wide enough to eat, so he had to take his sustenance through a straw. Turning Bolger into a scarecrow was also a miserable chore. Except

Lahr as the Cowardly Lion

for his eyes, his face was entirely covered by a plastic bag designed to reflect the Denslow drawings. It took an hour to apply and his costume involved another sixty minutes of careful application. When he was finally ready, he had to perform under the hot lights of the stage set and his body could not breath. If he stayed in the costume too long, he risked serious dehydration.

However, the worst problem awaited Buddy Ebsen. In order to transform him into the Tin Woodsman, it was necessary to dress him in a simulated tin suit, paste a tin hat onto his head, glue on a rubber nose and chin, coat his face with a white sticky paste, and then dust his face with powdered aluminum. Weeks into rehearsal, recording, and filming, Ebsen found himself in big trouble. At home one night, he started having difficulty breathing, and then a short time later he found himself gasping for air. He was rushed to the hospital, placed in the critical care ward, and put on a respirator. The diagnosis: His lungs were coated with aluminum dust that caused a severe allergic reaction. It took Ebsen two weeks of hospitalization and six weeks of rest to recover, and he was essentially out of action. MGM needed to find a new Tin Woodsman.

The job this time went to MGM contract player Jack Haley. Haley was far from enthusiastic about being a substitute performer in what he felt was a relatively minor role in a dubious film, but he had no choice.

Haley as the Tin Man

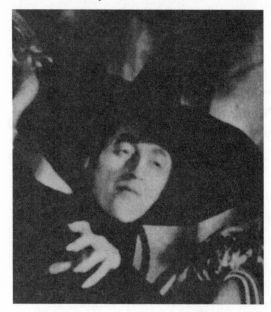

Hamilton as the Wicked Witch

He was fitted to Ebsen's costume with only minor changes and his makeup was identical, with one exception: Instead of using aluminum powder, the makeup experts colored his face with an aluminum paste. Haley survived the revised protocol with no difficulties.

There were other horrors ahead. Margaret Hamilton, in her role as the Wicked Witch, had an early scene in which she threatens Dorothy and then disappears in a burst of flame and red smoke. Everything went fine in rehearsal as she stepped back onto a small platform which dropped her down and out of sight as flames shot out from nearby jets. But when the time came for the live shot, the flames burst out prematurely, and Hamilton's broom and hat were set on fire. In a panic, stagehands extinguished the flames but not before she was seriously burned on her face and hand. Her makeup was carefully and painfully removed at the studio, her wounds were covered with salve, and she was sent home to recuperate. It was six weeks before she was able to work again.

On her first day back at the studio, Hamilton was being prepared for the scene in which she rides on her broomstick when she was told she would be using a fireproof costume. When she learned that her scene required smoke to emit from the broomstick she would be riding, Hamilton refused. There was no way she would risk fire again. As a result, her stand-in took her place. On the third take, the broomstick exploded, and Hamilton's replacement spent two weeks in recovery.

GETTING THE LITTLE PEOPLE READY

Then there were the Munchkins. Legend has it that many of them were drunks, that they had orgies in the hotels, and that they were quick to anger and hard to train. It was inevitable that the sudden assembly of more than a hundred little people, few of whom had any prior film experience, would create difficulties. But most of them were well behaved and serious about their work. The main problem was transporting, rehearsing, and costuming such a vast and varied group of unusual people. Each morning, busloads of Munchkins would arrive at the MGM gates, be shown to their rehearsal room, be measured for costumes, and be photographed by makeup. Each one had to have his or her specially made outfit, specially constructed nose and ears, and specially shaped felt shoes. They were taught their dances and moves in a huge staging hall, lined up in rows of thirty and forty. For each day of filming, all 124 Munchkins had to go through makeup. This was accomplished by setting up what amounted to a Munchkin makeup assembly line. Forty makeup chairs and forty makeup artists worked away, while the Munchkins moved on command from chair to chair for each phase of work on their faces. They came off the last chair ready to hop into their costumes and await their call to the set.

Since filming frequently lasted hours at a time, Munchkins frequently felt the call of nature. Because their costumes and shoes were not designed for locomotion, stagehands frequently carried them to the restrooms and then had to assist them in accomplishing their tasks. A Munchkin once fell into the toilet and wasn't retrieved until he was deemed missing some half an hour later. After that calamity, each Munchkin was helped on and off the toilet by an attendant.

Even Toto had her problems. She would sometimes fail to understand her assignment and ruin the shot. In the early scene when Dorothy starts down the Yellow Brick Road, Toto was supposed to be

The director with Garland and the Munchkins on set

in the lead. It required six takes before Toto got the message that she was supposed to lead and not follow. On a set where injury was a regular occurrence, Toto was not exempt. During the filming of the scene at the Emerald Castle, Toto was strolling in the midst of marching soldiers when one of the soldiers stepped on her and injured one of her legs. A stand-in for Toto was found and took the star's place until she recovered. Toto's trainer was certain that by the end of the filming the little dog was suffering a nervous breakdown.

THE DIRECTORS' REVOLVING DOOR

Almost from the outset, the "Oz" project suffered from an excess of leadership. Meryn LeRoy was a hands-on producer, involving himself in every phase of the film's progress. He shepherded the purchase of the film rights, hired and dismissed the succession of writers, supervised the casting, and fussed over every detail that came his way or that he could ferret out. Being the film's director under LeRoy would not be an easy task.

First to have a shot at the job was Richard Thorpe. Thorpe was an experienced MGM director with a number of successful films on his résumé. When LeRoy saw the first week's rushes, he was not happy. His first thought was that the actors were

Garland and some Munchkins
relaxing between scenes

letting him down and he called several of them into his office for a dressing down. When that didn't seem to improve things, he decided his director was the problem. Thorpe was fired after fewer than two weeks on the job.

LeRoy picked George Cukor to replace Thorpe. Cukor was considered a curious choice. Known for his success with actresses, he had directed Jean Harlow in *Dinner at Eight*, Norma Shearer in *Romeo and Juliet*, and Greta Garbo in *Camille*. Cukor's time would be limited because of a previously assigned commitment, but he quickly spotted the problem. Judy Garland had been made up like a substitute Shirley Temple—with a little-girl dress, a bow on her head, and a blond wig. Additionally, she had adopted a fey, childish way of speaking. Cukor realized that she had lost her authenticity as a simple girl from Kansas and the contrast that she should present to the fanciful world of Oz. Cukor restored her natural hair color, dressed her in a simple gingham dress, cleaned up her makeup, and instructed her to speak naturally. A few test scenes demonstrated the wisdom of the changes. Cukor had saved Dorothy—and probably the film. Cukor left the set and moved happily on to his next assignment.

10/31/38
Original Dress
own Hair & fall
before darkening

Judy Garland as Shirley Temple

With Cukor now gone, LeRoy thumbed through the MGM director's roster and came up with Victor Fleming. At first blush, Fleming seemed an even odder choice than Cukor. He was known in Hollywood as a "man's man" and as a director of male stars: Clark Gable in *Red Dust* and Spencer Tracy in *Captains Courageous*. The first thing Fleming did was to throw out all of the footage shot by Richard Thorpe. It had all been done with Garland's previous makeup and Fleming deemed it unusable. He was not completely happy with the script and called in yet another writer to reconstruct the opening and to repair other passages that did not seem to flow. Fleming was a taskmaster and a craftsman, and he set about making everything work and concentrated on getting the job done. He succeeded.

Once when Garland held up filming by getting the giggles over some of Bert Lahr's antics, Fleming gave her a good face slap to remind her of the task at hand. Within months, Fleming completed shooting all the Technicolor scenes in the Land of Oz, from Dorothy's arrival in the storm-tossed farmhouse to her return to Kansas via the magic ruby slippers. However, Fleming wasn't able to finish the film because David O. Selznick and *Gone with the Wind* got in the way. Selznick had fired George Cukor from his ambitious movie and, acquiescing to Clark Gable's request, asked for Fleming to take the director's place. Fleming scurried off to Selznick's studio, where he would achieve lasting fame and win an Academy Award as the director of the great Margaret Mitchell epic. King Vidor, yet another of MGM's stable of proven directors, became the fourth and last director of *The Wizard of Oz*, supervising the Kansas farm scenes that sandwiched Fleming's color footage. But, when all was said and done, it was Fleming's name that appeared that year as the director of two of the most famous movies ever made.

SAVING "OVER THE RAINBOW"

By mid-March of 1938, filming was finished. It had taken almost six months, cost more than $2 million, and survived eleven writers and four directors. More than five hundred people had performed in the filming. Over the next several months, the footage was submitted to sound augmentation and editing. In putting the film together, a number of minor errors were detected. In one of the opening scenes, Dorothy falls into a pigsty and miraculously emerges without a smudge on her dress. Dorothy's pigtails were different lengths in different scenes. In the scene when the trees threw apples at Dorothy, she is seen briefly wearing black shoes instead of ruby red. Several times, the shadow of a cameraman was visible on the screen, and once the wire holding up the Cowardly Lion's tail could be seen. None of these minor glitches was deemed serious enough to call the cast back for reshooting.

The film was previewed before a live audience in a theater in San Bernardino in June and the audience was enthusiastic; it loved Judy's Dorothy, hissed at the Wicked Witch, and responded favorably to the three comic characters. But there was a problem: The film ran close to two hours, longer than most audiences were accustomed to and longer than theater managers liked. Something had to give. Painfully, an entire dance and singing sequence called "The Jitterbug" was excised. It had taken five weeks to film and cost the studio $80,000. It had featured some of Ray Bolger's finest work, but taking it out saved almost five minutes of running time. Many of Hamilton's best lines as the Wicked Witch were expunged. Then Louis B. Mayer himself insisted on another cut: He wanted "Over the Rainbow" removed from the opening sequence.

Usually when Mayer wanted something done at MGM, it was done without question. He was the supreme boss of the studio and

Off to see the Wizard

not accustomed to being challenged or defied. But for songwriters Harold Arlen and Yip Harburg, this was a special case. They knew the importance of the song to the movie and to their own careers. They confronted Mayer and explained how critical the song was to portray Dorothy's longing for something better in her life—and to segue into the dreamworld that was the heart and bulk of the film. Mayer countered that he didn't think the song was anything special, that it slowed down the film, that it took too much time, and that there was no logic in Dorothy singing such a romantic song standing in a barnyard. The disagreement went on for some time, with "Over the Rainbow" hanging in the balance. Finally, Arthur Freed, the assistant director and MGM's musical maven, interceded on the songwriters' behalf and Mayer reluctantly gave in. The song would stay—and music lovers would be rewarded for decades to come. Mayer did, however, achieve one minor victory on the subject: The reprise of "Over the Rainbow" at the end of the movie was axed.

THE PEOPLE VERSUS THE CRITICS

The Wizard of Oz premiered on the West Coast at Grauman's Chinese Theater on August 15, 1939, and, two days later, at Loew's Capitol Theater in New York. Audiences, often dominated by children, sat mesmerized during the film and cheered when it was over. When the film was generally released in major cities across the country on August 25, it attracted large and enthusiastic audiences. And it brought in money: In the first week, the box office receipts were almost $100,000, and, before its initial run was complete, *The Wizard of Oz* grossed more than $3 million. Critics tended to be less enthusiastic and some of them were downright caustic. Wrote The *New Republic*: "*The Wizard of Oz* was intended to hit the same audience of *Snow White* and won't fail for lack of trying … It can't be expected to have a sense of humor—and as for the light torch of fantasy, it weighs like a pound of fruitcake soaking wet." The *New Yorker* whined, "Fantasy is still Walt Disney's domain … I sat cringing before MGM's production of *The Wizard of Oz*, which displays no sense of imagination, good taste, or integrity." *McCall's* lamented, "the evil witch chasing the little girl all around the castle … as though

the girl were a gangster and the witch and her cohorts a band of G-men."
Critic Russell Maloney simply described the film as "a stinkeroo."

Some reviewers were kinder, particularly at the local level, and it
was up to The *New York Times* to turn the tables on the film's harsher
critics: "It is so well-intentioned, so genial, so gay that any reviewer who
would look down his nose at the fun-making should be spanked and
sent off, supperless, to bed."

THE PASSAGE OF TIME

Even after a full year had passed, MGM still didn't know what to make
of *The Wizard of Oz*. Despite its credible box office numbers, the film
had not really been profitable. After its initial runs, "Oz" had grossed
just over $3 million, but the film had been the most costly production
in MGM history. When all the costs of production, distribution, and
promotion were totaled up, the movie lost almost a million dollars for
the studio. It had been planned from the outset as a prestige film, but
reviews had been mixed at best. Nominated for six Academy Awards,
including Best Picture, but caught in the downdraft of *Gone with the
Wind*, it won only two awards, for Best Song and Best Original Score,
along with a special award for Judy Garland. *The Wizard of Oz* had
not been a failure—but neither had it been a great success. With its
reputation in limbo, the movie was reluctantly consigned to the MGM
storage vaults, where it would reside for the next ten years.

AFTER THE WIZARD OF OZ

Judy Garland was established as a Hollywood megastar with her
triumphal appearance in "Oz." She quickly appeared with Mickey
Rooney in three more Andy Hardy films and then starred in a series
of extraordinary MGM musical films, including *For Me and My Gal*,
Meet Me in St. Louis, *Till the Clouds Roll By*, *Ziegfeld Follies*, and *Words
and Music*. But Garland's increasingly erratic behavior, fueled by alcohol
and drugs, cost her important roles. She started but was removed from
such films as *Royal Wedding* (replaced by June Allyson), *Annie Get Your
Gun* (replaced by Betty Hutton), and *The Barkleys of Broadway* (replaced

by Ginger Rogers). She was finally suspended and her contract was canceled by MGM in 1950.

A year later, Garland began a second career on the stage, performing to great acclaim as a solo performer in shows at the Palace Theater in New York and the Palladium in London. The following year, she took another movie assignment in Warner Brothers' *A Star Is Born* and was nominated for an Academy Award for her outstanding performance. Over the next dozen years, Garland alternated between stage performances, television appearances, and movie assignments. She appeared in *Judgment at Nuremberg*, *A Child Is Waiting*, and *I Could Go on Singing*, her last film role.

Garland had a chaotic love life, involving many affairs, and she married five times. With husband Vincente Minnelli, she had a daughter Liza, who later became a singing and acting star in her own right. Garland's health continued to deteriorate and she was found dead in her London hotel room in 1969, the victim of alcohol and of a prescription drug overdose. She was forty-seven years old. Ray Bolger, her "Oz" costar, said at her funeral, "Judy just plain wore out."

In 1999, the American Film Institute named Judy Garland one of the "Greatest Female Stars of All Time."

✻ ✻ ✻

Ray Bolger resumed his stage career after "Oz," performing with the Harry James orchestra at the Paramount Theater in New York. During World War II, he toured in USO shows, entertaining the troops, and appeared in the wartime film *Stage Door Canteen*. He returned to MGM in 1946 and starred in *The Harvey Girls*. His first love, however, was the stage, where he could take advantage of his singing and dancing skills. His later Broadway credits include *Life Begins at 8:40*, *On Your Toes*, and *By Jupiter*. His most acclaimed performance was in *Where's Charley?*, for which he won a Tony Award. He subsequently made a film version of the show and traveled the country for more than a decade performing the role of "Charley." He made a number of television appearances, including two seasons in *The Ray Bolger Show*. He continued to appear in films, most notably in Walt Disney's *Babes in Toyland*. He was a regular on the

Sheet music of
"Over the Rainbow"

Garland singing in an
Oz recording session

television series *The Partridge Family* and *Little House on the Prairie*, and he continued to be active into his eighties in both films and television.

Bolger died in 1987 at the age of eighty-four. He was, at the time, the last living member of the cast of *The Wizard of Oz*. Mysteriously, his official obituary made no mention of the film.

Bert Lahr returned to the stage after "Oz," starring in a succession of musicals, including *DuBarry Was a Lady*, *The Seven Lively Arts*, and *Burlesque*. His most celebrated role on Broadway was in *Waiting for Godot*, Samuel Beckett's revolutionary stage play. Lahr later claimed that he had no idea what Beckett's play was about. He continued to appear in films and on television shows through the 1950s and '60s and died in 1967 during the filming of *The Night They Raided Minsky's*. His costume as the Cowardly Lion resides in the Comisar Collection, the world's largest collection of television/movie artifacts. It has been valued at $1.5 million.

Audiences cheering at a viewing of *The Wizard of Oz*

Following his role as the Tin Man, Jack Haley continued to make movie musicals and comedies. Among his subsequent film credits are *Moon Over Miami*, *Beyond the Blue Horizon*, *George White's Scandals*, and *New York, New York*. In all, Haley appeared in thirty-six motion pictures for MGM and RKO Radio Pictures. He died in 1979 at the age of eighty, just one week after appearing with Ray Bolger at the Academy Awards in a salute to the fortieth anniversary of *The Wizard of Oz*.

Frank Morgan won high praise for his role as the Wizard and was in great demand as a character actor for the next decade. He appeared in an additional thirty movies, seldom as a star, but almost always providing memorable performances. Morgan was the first of the "Oz" stars to leave the scene, dying of a heart attack just ten years after the filming of *The Wizard of Oz*. He never lived to see the film's extraordinary popularity on television.

Margaret Hamilton, despite a movie career that included more than seventy-five films, remained famous for the rest of her life as Oz's Wicked Witch. Children would frequently come up to her and ask her why she had been so mean to Dorothy. She often appeared before groups of grade school students to emphasize the importance of education, and she was invariably asked to do her cackling witch's laugh. Hamilton told her biographer that it almost always got the same reaction: It scared them all over again.

Terry, the little dog who played Toto, quickly recovered from the trauma of the "Oz" filming. She became so famous as a result of that role that her owner changed her name to "Toto," and she appeared in thirteen more movies. She died in 1947 at the age of eleven and is remembered by a permanent memorial at the Hollywood Forever Cemetery in Los Angeles.

✻ ✻ ✻

The Wizard of Oz was rereleased to the nation's theaters during the 1948–1949 season, and the film brought in another $1.5 million in revenue, making the film profitable for the first time. However, it was not until its appearance on television that it hit the jackpot. While overall profitability is difficult to determine, it is believed that MGM's subsequent owners, Ted Turner and Warner Brothers, have realized the principal rewards from the film's popularity. Viewing *The Wizard of Oz* on television at Halloween time has become almost a rite-of-passage for youngsters.

"Over the Rainbow" became the most recorded popular song of the twentieth century.

Poster for *The Wizard of Oz*

THE WIZARD OF OZ
THE FINAL FACTS

Studio:	Metro-Goldwyn-Mayer
Executive Producer:	Mervyn LeRoy
Director:	Victor Fleming
Screenplay:	Noel Langley, Florence Ryerson, Edgar Allan Wolf
Original Story:	L. Frank Baum
Cinematography:	Harold Rosson
Music:	Herbert Stothart (score), Harold Arlen and E. Y. "Yip" Harburg (songs)
Release Date:	August 25, 1939
Running Time:	101 minutes
Cost of Production:	$2,777,000
Box Office (original run):	$3,017,000
Estimated total revenue:	$175,000,000

Cast

Dorothy Gale	Judy Garland
The Wizard	Frank Morgan
Tin Man	Jack Haley
Scarecrow	Ray Bolger
Cowardly Lion	Bert Lahr
Good Witch of the North	Billie Burke
Wicked Witch of the West	Margaret Hamilton
Aunt Em	Clara Blandick
Uncle Henry	Charley Grapewin
Munchkins	The Singer Midgets and others
Toto	Terry

Awards

Academy Award Nominations: Best Picture, Best Special Effects, Best Original Score, Best Song, Best Color Cinematography, Best Art Direction.

Academy Awards Won: Judy Garland, Special Award; Herbert Stothart for Best Original Score; Harold Arlen and E. Y. "Yip" Harburg for Best Song.

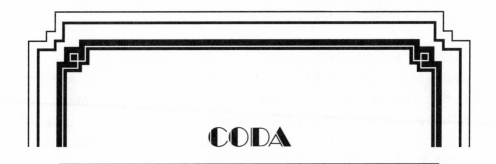

CODA

This book has taken an in-depth look at how, in one year, six great stories were adapted and translated into memorable motion pictures. But there were other works of literature that were made into excellent films in 1939. Some waited decades, others only a few years, to make their film debut. Following are brief descriptions of twelve of special note.

BEAU GESTE

English author P. C. Wren's 1924 novel about British family values and adventures in the French Foreign Legion was one of the most popular books of its time. In 1939, Paramount turned the story into a major motion picture with William A. Wellman producing and directing. Its all-star cast included Gary Cooper, Susan Hayward, Broderick Crawford, Brian Donlevy, and Robert Preston. The film was popular with both critics and moviegoers. It was nominated for Best Art Direction, an award that went to *Gone with the Wind*.

DRUMS ALONG THE MOHAWK

American novelist Walter D. Edmonds published his story about life on the early American frontier in 1936, and it became an instant popular hit. It stayed on the best-seller list for three years with thirty-three reprintings. In 1939 it became a major motion picture, starring Henry Fonda, Claudette Colbert, Ward Bond, and John Carradine. It was one of four pictures directed by John Ford that year, and it was well received by both the critics and the public. It was nominated by the Academy for Best Supporting Actress and Best Color Photography, losing out on both to *Gone with the Wind*.

THE FOUR FEATHERS

British writer A. E. W. Mason's 1902 adventure novel was set in 1880s Egypt and told the story of both heroism and cowardice among the ruling British forces. United Artists turned the story into a lavishly filmed production that featured settings shot on location in the Sudan. Ralph Richardson played the dashing English military hero, while C. Aubrey Smith lent an air of upper-class British snobbery to the events. The movie was nominated for Best Color Photography which went, inevitability, to *Gone with the Wind*.

GOODBYE, MR. CHIPS

British writer James Hilton's 1937 novel told the story of the headmaster of a traditional English boy's school, chronicling his life from the time he was a young teacher until he became the revered headmaster of the school. The book's instant popularity inspired MGM to purchase the film rights and put some of its major talent into a film version. Robert Donat was selected to play Mr. Chips and Greer Garson was given her first major role as his young wife. The movie was a critical and financial success and was nominated for seven Academy Awards. It won only one, when Robert Donat's Mr. Chips edged out Clark Gable's Rhett Butler for Best Actor.

GUNGA DIN

Rudyard Kipling in 1890 published his celebrated poem about the heroism of a native Indian water boy who saves the life of a British soldier. Writers Ben Hecht, Charles MacArthur, and William Faulkner created a film adaptation of the story for RKO Radio Pictures. With a superb cast headed by Cary Grant and Douglas Fairbanks Jr., George Stevens created a highly entertaining film, filled with adventure, spectacle, and sterling performances. It became the second-highest grossing film of the year, surpassed only by *Gone with the Wind*.

THE HUNCHBACK OF NOTRE DAME

Victor Hugo's classic novel, *Notre Dame de Paris*, about fifteenth-century Paris, was published in 1831. A 1923 silent film based on the book starred Lon Chaney, but the first sound and major film version was produced by RKO Radio Pictures in 1939. Charles Laughton played the lead role as Quasimodo, with Maureen O'Hara, Thomas Mitchell, and Edmond O'Brien in supporting roles. It was favorably reviewed by the nation's critics and was nominated for two Academy Awards. It was not surprising that it lost out to *Gone with the Wind*.

THE LITTLEST PRINCESS

In 1905 Frances Hodgson Burnett wrote a classic children's novel called *The Littlest Princess*, considered to be one of the one hundred best children's stories of all time. It is a heartwarming tale about a young girl relegated to servitude in a boarding house after her father is believed to be dead. Twentieth Century Fox decided it would be the perfect vehicle for their number-one box office star, Shirley Temple. Produced by Gene Markey and directed by Walter Lang, it turned out to be Temple's last great film success. The film was well reviewed and did well financially, but it marked the essential end of one of the most legendary careers in movie history.

THE MAN IN THE IRON MASK

The last third of a monumental novel by Alexandre Dumas is called *The Man in the Iron Mask*. It takes up the legend that the illegitimate brother of Louis XIV of France was imprisoned in the Bastille for thirty-four years, and that his identity was unknown because his face was encased in an iron mask. A glamorized version of the tale was put on the screen in 1939 by United Artists. The film starred Louis Hayward, Joan Bennett, and a host of lesser-known contract players. The film was reviewed as "moderately entertaining" and did not do well at the box office.

Of Mice and Men
John Steinbeck's 1937 novel was a morality tale about two itinerant workers—Lennie, a simple-minded giant who did not know his own strength, and George, Lennie's smaller companion, who must kill him to save him from himself. United Artists took on the task of translating this difficult book into film, giving Lon Chaney Jr. the role of Lennie and Burgess Meredith the role of George. A critical success, the film was profitable on its initial run and was nominated for Best Picture and in two other categories, losing in all three.

The Rains Came
Louis Bromfield's sprawling 1937 novel was an epic bestseller requiring more than thirty reprints in its first year. It was a love story that featured a romantic triangle between a British woman, her lover, and an Indian doctor. The film starred Myrna Loy and Tyrone Power in the leading roles, and it portrayed a series of natural calamities, including flood, earthquake, plague, and fire. Its dramatic visual effects won the 1939 Academy Award for Special Effects for Twentieth Century Fox.

Wuthering Heights
Emily Bronte's famous story of desperate love and tragic revenge was published in mid-nineteenth-century England. Despite a 1920 British film adaptation, it did not come fully to cinematic life until Sam Goldwyn Productions gave the project to screenwriter Ben Hecht and director William Wyler. The result was a winning screenplay and a well-directed film starring Laurence Olivier as Heathcliff and Merle Oberon as Catherine. The New York Film Critics named it the Best Picture of the Year, edging out the otherwise invincible *Gone with the Wind*.

The Women
Playwright Clare Booth's long-running play *The Women* ran for almost two years on Broadway before MGM put it in the hands of a succession of different screenwriters, including F. Scott Fitzgerald. The result was a George Cukor–directed film that starred a host of female screen luminaries, including Joan Crawford, Paulette Goddard, Joan Fontaine,

Ruth Hussey, and Norma Shearer. Director Cukor was available because he had been fired off the set of *Gone with the Wind*. The film was one of the great financial successes of 1939.

As of its publication, all of the movies described in this book were seen for the first time seventy-five years ago. They pleased, thrilled, and excited moviegoers then—and they still bring pleasure to people who see them today. Viewed against today's motion pictures, they may seem simplistic, even quaint. But together they represent a remarkable advance in film art. If any of these films strikes your fancy or piques your interest, you should take a look. My guess is that you will find yourself mesmerized by the art and craft of moviemaking at its finest during Hollywood's Golden Age.

BIBLIOGRAPHY

GONE WITH THE WIND

The chapter on *Gone with the Wind* was written using information and quotations taken from the two definitive works on the making of the film: *Scarlett, Rhett*, by Roland Fanini, Collier Macmillan Publishers, Inc., NY, 1973; and *Gone with the Wind*, by Herb Bridges and Terrence C. Boodman, Simon & Schuster, NY, 1989.

Also useful were *Selznick*, by Bob Thomas, Doubleday, NY, 1997; *Margaret Mitchell of Atlanta*, by Finis Farr, William Morrow, NY, 1957; *Hollywood in the Thirties*, by John Baxter, Paperback Library, NY, 1970; *Hollywood Rajah*, by Bosley Crowther, Holt, Rinehart and Winston, NY, 1960; *1939: The Year in Movies*, by Tom Flannery, McFarland & Company, Inc., NY, 1990; *Gable and Lombard*, by Warren G. Harris, Simon & Schuster, NY, 1974; and *The Road to Tara*, by Aljean Harmetz, H. N. Abrams, NY, 1996.

STAGECOACH

The chapter on *Stagecoach* was based on the following sources: *The Life of Ernest Haycox*, by Ernest Haycox, Jr., University of Oklahoma Press, 2003; *Ernest Haycox*, by Stephen L. Tanner, Twayne Publishers, NY, 1996; *John Ford: The Man and His Films*, by Tag Gallagher, University of California Press, 1986; *John Wayne: American*, by Randy Roberts and James S. Olson, University of Nebraska Press, 1951; *John Ford's Stagecoach*, edited by Barry Keith Grant, Cambridge University Press, 2003; *The Young Duke*, by Howard Kazanjian and Chris Enss, Globe

Pequot Press, Guilford, CT, 2009; *John Wayne: The Man Behind the Myth*, by Michael Munn, New American Library, NY, 2003; *John Ford Made Westerns*, edited by Gaylin Studlar and Matthew Bernstein, Indiana University Press, 2001; *John Ford's Stagecoach*, edited by Richard J. Anobile, Flare Books, NY, 1975.

Mr. Smith Goes to Washington

The chapter on *Mr. Smith Goes to Washington* takes much of its information from *The Name Above the Title*, by Frank Capra, The Macmillan Company, NY, 1971; *Jimmy Stewart: A Life in Film*, by Roy Pickard, St. Martin's Press, NY, 1992; *Jean Arthur: The Actress Nobody Knew*, by John Oller, Limelight Editions, NY, 1997; *Hollywood 1930s*, by Jack Lodge, Gallery Books, NY, 1985; *Columbia Pictures: The Story of a Studio*, by Bernard F. Dick, University Press of Kentucky, Lexington, KY, 1992; *The Columbia Story*, by Clive Hirschhorn, Crown, NY, 1990; *The Pictures of Frank Capra*, by Donald C. Willis, Scarecrow Press, NJ, 1974; and *The Merchant Prince of Poverty Row: Harry Cohn of Columbia Pictures*, by Bernard F. Dick, University Press of Kentucky, Lexington, KY, 2009.

The Hound of the Baskervilles

The chapter on *The Hound of the Baskervilles* was derived from a number of authoritative sources: *A Biography of Arthur Conan Doyle*, by Martin Booth, Harden & Stroughton Publishing, London, 1997; *In and Out of Character*, by Basil Rathbone, Doubleday, Garden City, NY, 1962; *Holmes of the Movies*, by David Stuart Davies, Bramhall House, NY 1968; *The Hound of the Baskervilles*, by Sir Arthur Conan Doyle, Harper & Collins, NY, 2008; *1939: The Year in Movies*, by Tom Flannery, McFarland & Company, Inc., Jefferson, NC, 1990; *The Life and Times of Sherlock Holmes*, by Christopher Roden, Crescent Books, NY, 1992; and *The Ultimate Sherlock Holmes Encyclopedia*, by Jack Tracy, Random House, NY, 1977.

The Adventures of Huckleberry Finn

The chapter on *The Adventures of Huckleberry Finn* is based on the following sources: *Huckleberry Finn on Film*, by Clyde V. Haupt, McFarland & Co., NY, 1994; *Life Is Too Short*, by Mickey Rooney, Villard Books, NY, 1991; *Mark Twain: A Life*, by Ron Powers, Free Press, NY, 2006; *Mark Twain: God's Fool*, by Hamlin Hill, Harper & Row, NY, 1973; *The Adventures of Huckleberry Finn on Film*, by Frank Perry, Des Plains Publishers, Greenwood, IL, 1985; *The Adventures of Huckleberry Finn*, by Mark Twain, University of California Press, 2003; *The Singular Mark Twain*, by Fred Kaplan, Doubleday, NY, 2003.

The Wizard of Oz

The chapter on *The Wizard of Oz* is based on information from *L. Frank Baum, Creator of Oz*, by Katherine M. Rogers, Da Capo Press, Cambridge, MA, 2002; *The Making of The Wizard of Oz*, by Aljean Harmetz, Hyperion, NY, 1977; *The Wonderful Wizard of Oz*, by Frank Baum, Signet Classics, NY, 2006; *The MGM Story*, by John D. Eames, Crown, NY, 1975; *Victor Fleming: An American Movie Master*, by Michael Sragow, Pantheon, NY, 2008; *Judy*, by Gerald Frank, Harper & Row, NY, 1972; *Mervyn LeRoy: Take One*, by Mervyn LeRoy, Hawthorne Publishers, NY, 1997; *Notes on a Cowardly Lion*, by John Lahr, Alfred A. Knopf, NY, 1969; and *Oz Before the Rainbow*, by Mark Evan Swart, Johns Hopkins University Press, Baltimore, 2000.

INDEX

Laugh harder and live longer with these great books

California Fruits, Flakes, and Nuts
True Tales of California Crazies, Crackpots, and Creeps
by David Kulczyk

From insane celebrities to wacky religious cults, if it's weird, it happens in California. A freewheeling catalog of misfits, eccentrics, creeps, criminals and failed dreamers, *California Fruits, Flakes, and Nuts* relates the hilarious and heartbreaking lives of 48 bizarre personalities who exemplify California's well-deserved reputation for nonconformity. It's a side-splitting, shocking, and salacious salute to the people who made California the strangest place on earth.

$14.95 ($16.95 Canada)

Sitting Kills, Moving Heals
How Simple Everyday Movement Will Prevent Pain, Illness, and Early Death—and Exercise Alone Won't
by Joan Vernikos, Ph.D., former Director of NASA's Life Sciences Division

New medical research has shown that sitting too much will shorten your life, even if you get regular exercise. *Sitting Kills, Moving Heals* shows that the key to lifelong fitness and good health is constant, nonstrenuous movement that resists the force of gravity. This easy-to-follow, common-sense plan will show you how simple, everyday, and fun activities like walking, gardening, dancing, golf, and more will keep you fit, strong and independent your whole life long.

$14.95 ($16.95 Canada)

ABOUT THE AUTHOR

Charles F. Adams spent his career in international marketing and was President and Chief Operating Officer of D'Arcy, MacManus and Masius, Inc., one of the world's largest advertising agencies. Now retired, he continues to serve as Chairman of the Wajim Corporation and President of Adams Enterprises. He is also a former owner and general partner of the Pittsburgh Penguins of the National Hockey League. He has chaired a number of charitable and civic organizations.

Adams' previous books include *Common Sense in Advertising* (McGraw-Hill, 1968), *Heroes of the Golden Gate* (Pacific Books, 1987), *California in the Year 2000* (Pacific Books, 1991), *The Magnificent Rogues* (Pacific Books, 1998), *Murder by the Bay* (Craven Street Books, 2005), and *The Complete Geezer Guidebook* (Quill Driver Books, 2009).

Adams has written a number of plays which have been performed in San Francisco, where he lives.